CV00905085

THE LITTLE BOOK OF INSPIRATIONAL TEACHING ACTIVITIES

Bringing NLP into the Classroom

David Hodgson Edited by Ian Gilbert

Crown House Publishing Limited
www.crownhouse.co.uk – www.crownhousepublishing.com

First published by

Crown House Publishing Ltd
Crown Buildings, Bancyfelin, Carmarthen,
Wales, SA33 5ND, UK
www.crownhouse.co.uk

and

Crown House Publishing Company LLC
6 Trowbridge Drive, Suite 5, Bethel, CT 06801, USA
www.crownhousepublishing.com

First published 2009. Reprinted 2009, 2010.

British Library Cataloguing-in-Publication Data A catalogue entry for this book is available from the British Library.

ISBN 978-184590136-3   LCCN 2008936821

Printed and bound in the UK by
Gomer Press, Llandysul, Ceredigion

Dedicated to Jonty, John and Jason

Contents

Foreword

An academic, a psychologist and an NLP practitioner walked into a bar. While they're there they have a discussion about NLP. The academic dismisses it outright as there is no specific academic research to back up its claims about helping people communicate better, understand each other better and get more out of everyone including ourselves. The psychologist also dismisses it, claiming that it is a pseudoscience using pseudoscientific language to pretend to be something that no-one has proved it is. The NLP practitioner, meanwhile, is enjoying his pint and has just managed to get a date with the girl behind the bar.

Whatever it isn't, what NLP is is a fascinating way of experimenting with language, with communication, with thinking and with interactions that, regardless of what the theorists may say, does make a tangible difference in the real world (whatever that is as we all have different ones).

NLP or Neuro-Linguistic Programming (and here the psychologist may have a point) grew out of the work of academic linguist John Grinder and student Richard Bandler in California in the 1970s. They were looking at the language and strategies employed by three great therapists, Fritz Perls, Virginia Satir and Milton Erickson. Picking through hours of video and audio tapes of therapy sessions led by these three, one of the things that Bandler and Grinder identified was that there were just three main patterns of behaviour that could be found in successful communication:

To know what you want.
To be flexible enough to try different things to achieve it.
To have enough 'sensory acuity' to notice what is happening when it is.

From these early roots the huge sprawling empire that is NLP was born, spawning a thousand copyists and a million acolytes and more than just a handful of people who are very scathing about the whole thing.

For teachers who have not heard of NLP, be aware that the whole world of 'VAK' teaching and learning comes from it. This is the idea that when we take ideas into our head from the outside world they can only come in through our senses and, putting olfactory and gustatory to one side for most, if not all, classes, that means we must help people learn in *visual*, *auditory* and *kinaesthetic* ways. Good multi-sensory learning is not too controversial but the idea that we have a *preferred* way of learning across VAK does cause the academic theorists to get a bit agitated in their seats. Where some schools have taken it to an illogical extreme: 'I'm a kinaesthetic learner so don't ask me to listen to you as I'll be too busy playing with this koosh ball.' I have seen it all too often where the child struggling to understand a concept in one 'modality', say by the teacher *telling* them it, gets it immediately when *shown* it or *physically* representing it.

Dave Hodgson has been successfully using NLP for many years to help young people get a little closer to their potential. What he has put together in this handy 'Little Book' is a collection of powerful but simple ideas, strategies and exercises that allow anyone to draw on some of the best elements of NLP and get the most out of their own students in the classroom and beyond.

Artfully arranged as set of playing cards with themes based around the four suits, a teacher armed with this book can immediately get to grips with NLP in the classroom and make their own conclusions about how effective it is as a tool for communication and inspiration.

And remember, as was once famously said, 'The map is not the territory'. NLP may not exist, but it works.

Ian Gilbert, Suffolk
March 2009

Preface

The little book of big pants?

I had an idea for an activity. I went into British Home Stores and hung around the bra and pants section, plucking up the courage to study the knickers on display. I didn't realise there was such a wide choice. Determined not to make eye contact with anyone, I focused on the pants. Then I saw what I was after. In the same way that a bride knows she has found the ideal wedding dress, I realised they were the ladies' pants for me. I took three pairs of size 22 in pink, white and green. That's a lot of 100% cotton for just £5. I hurried across to the counter and handed them over, thankful there was not a long queue. As the middle-aged lady assistant peered over the rim of her glasses to get a better look at me, I was reading her mind, 'It's OK,' I said helpfully, 'they're for my work.' I had hoped this would make it seem less odd, but I think it just made things worse. The next day I delivered a session to a group of students. I told the story of my shopping experience and then explained the game:

> I divided them into three teams. When the music started they were to take turn in putting on the pants. But – and here's the twist – they had to do it wrong. Their task was to discover as many incorrect ways of putting on the pants as they could while the music played. And so they did, to the theme music from *Benny Hill*. Once each person had managed about three goes I stopped the music.

This exercise was inspired by watching my 3-year-old daughter getting ready in the morning. Could there really be that many wrong ways to put on a pair of pants? In preparing for the session I had come up with 12, but I hadn't thought of using arms and head as well as legs. The students were far more creative. How did they feel after the activity? 'Great,' they said, 'it was fun.' It's OK to be silly if everyone else is joining in; the thought of doing something potentially embarrassing is worse than actually doing it.

And the point of the whole pants exercise? – Leaving a group of teenage children with the feeling of being motivated, of believing in themselves and knowing that, if they wanted to, they could go for it. Not a bad result for a three-pack of big ladies' smalls.

(In fact, the session and this activity went so well, the teacher suggested I put all the materials together. Which is why you're now reading this book.)

Introduction

The mediocre teacher tells.
The good teacher explains.
The superior teacher demonstrates.
The great teacher inspires.

William Arthur Ward

I'm delighted that this book is being published as part of the *Independent Thinking Series* of Little Books. I used to think only Stephen Fry or the BBC could save Britain from itself. Now I think it's up to teachers and people such as myself who are doing our best to blaze a trail. Richard Bandler, co-founder of Neuro Linguistic Programming, has said, 'There is no such thing as learning disabilities, just teaching disabilities.' Before you throw down this book in disdain, with a Jeremy-Paxman-interviewing-a-politician look on your face, don't worry. This isn't about slating teachers. There's enough of that already. 'Respec' to da teachers' I say. I genuinely believe the only way we can change the world is by changing the way we teach children.

Independent Thinking Ltd is doing to the curriculum what Jamie Oliver did to turkey twizzlers. The challenge is to convince all of the brilliant teachers out there to believe in themselves as much as they believe in their students. I'm looking forward to the day teachers strike – not for extra pay but because they don't want to let the politicians mess up education anymore. Fire fighters did this a few years ago and received massive public support.

John Taylor Gatto, a teacher for over 30 years, writes eloquently about the need for a rethink on education in his book *Dumbing Us Down*. He describes the real curriculum obscured by the sound bites and pronouncements from politicians, business people and religious groups. It makes uncomfortable yet enlightening reading and I consider it a call to arms for teachers. It has inspired me to put together this collection of activities.

3

Did you see that programme about naturism?

A rather pleasant, plump, middle-aged woman, wearing only her handbag, was being interviewed by the pool. She remarked that most naturists were, physically, 'nothing much to look at.' The evidence – assorted middle-aged naked people milling around the pool or splashing in it – supported her observation. She went on to assert that younger people don't enjoy naturism when their bodies are at their best because their confidence is at its lowest. What would the world be like if it were the other way round? Listening to this woman, with rapt attention, I had two thoughts. First, isn't education about building and boosting young people's confidence so they can be and do their best? Second, can sitting naked on slatted plastic garden furniture really be comfortable?

The purpose of this book is to provide you with 62 activities designed to inspire people to be their best. So come with me. The activities are described succinctly on a series of playing cards and many require little or no preparation.

They adhere to the following Rules of Inspiration:

The Rules of Inspiration

They RING!

For an activity to work, it should be Relevant, Interesting, Naughty or a Giggle. If they are all four you're really chiming.

If you're not sure whether an activity is relevant, put yourself in the shoes of your audience and ask the 'WIIFM?' question, 'What's in it for me?' What do the students gain from listening and taking part? Are they clear about the gain?

You can judge whether it is interesting or not by measuring the response of the students. Do they sigh with boredom when you introduce the lesson, or sigh in disappointment when it ends?

'Naughty' is not about content but about the style and construction of the session. We learn and remember better if we are taken out of our comfort zones. The number one question astronauts are asked by adults and children is about 'number twos'!

You don't need to be a stand-up comedian to have a giggle; use the humour from within the group. If it is relaxed and engaged, humour will flow automatically from unexpected places and make your session unique and memorable.

For more on these simple but effective tips on motivating and inspiring your students, plunge into Ian Gilbert's *Essential Motivation in the Classroom*.

They can be made into stories

A good session is like a perfectly balanced five-course meal; all parts complementing each other to create a satisfying whole. The least satisfying meals I've encountered are buffet leftovers, uncon-nected and unbalanced cold items usually including enough scotch eggs to sustain a class of Year 11 boys for a month. This book can be used in the following ways:

- Select individual card activities to complement or refresh your existing sessions.
- Create full sessions using a collection of cards. The suits and numbers can act as a guide. One activity from each suit, in the sequence followed (diamonds, hearts, clubs then spades) and the same number provide a coherent session including a consistent theme using a range of activity styles (for example the 3 of diamonds and 3 of hearts both use a parachuting metaphor and if followed by the 3 of clubs and 3 of spades allow students to use a wide range of learning styles).
- For Inset.

Suggested combinations of activities are provided in Part Two of this book. The activities are written mostly with teacher and their students in mind but are suitable for all trainers and professionals working with teenagers. The text alongside each card provides ideas on how to adapt and develop each activity. The card description is a clear description of the activity itself.

A story I've heard a few times in NLP circles is the one about the elephant chained by the leg to a post from an early age that learned to move only the short distance the tether would allow. It became so conditioned that, as an adult, it would only move within the same area, even though the chain was no longer capable of restraining the strength of an elephant and it was no longer attached to the post anyway. Despite being bigger and stronger than its captors the elephant was trapped within the boundary it perceived as real. The story ticks a number of NLP boxes. Which ones? Well, when I deliver presentation skills training, delegates give a short discourse that has to start, 'If there's one thing in life I've learned it's ...' They are not allowed to say what the one thing is. At the end we ask each person in the audience what they thought the message was. What's fascinating is that they all have a different interpretation – interestingly, an interpretation that is best suited to their own lives and situation. A version of the elephant story, using a bird illustration, appears on the bottom right corner of each page of this book. Flick the pages quickly and the bird appears to be caged; slow down and you see it is able to fly ... if it wants to.

They apply learning theory and research

The best bits of NLP are drawn together through activities: accelerated learning, multiple intelligences, brain development, memory techniques, coaching, and even illusionist Derren Brown. I know that many people regard NLP as a bunch of odd people jousting with jargon. But for me, NLP has as much to do with intellectual jousting as Victoria Beckham has to do with Gordon Brown, and unless there is a juicy scandal around the corner, I don't think the two are meant to be together.

The voices of those questioning the way we educate our children are becoming louder. They're going to have to speak up.

*The education system we have is perfectly suited
for the needs of the century we're in.*

This statement may have been true if I were writing in 1850.

*Politicians are either clueless or too scared
to make the changes needed.*

This statement tends to be true in whatever year you write it.

The best theories are often beautifully clear and balanced, such as
the double helix structure of DNA. The premise of this book – find
meaning in your life through a cycle of four steps that allow you
to explore the world within you and around you – is also easy to
understand. Putting it into practice can be tricky.

Maintaining a healthy weight is not really complicated. The Billy
Connolly diet is 'eat less, move more'. Beautifully simple. It wouldn't
make a book though, with just four words. Even poetry books and
books with pictures have loads more words than that. So the advice
is straightforward, the practice needs a little work.

These steps seem to be used by all the successful people who are
prepared to share their methods, and probably many people who
don't. I've looked all over for the meaning of life. Philosophy? No
deal. Science? Religion? You're having a laugh. Pop music is the
source of the best wisdom and advice. And not just the Beatles and
Morrissey; even the much-derided Eurovision Song Contest delivers
more answers than the most beardy academics. In fact, I can prove
it. In an activity I use with adults and young people I ask, 'Imagine
your life in five years time as if you are at your absolute best'. They
list their achievements and I ask, 'What advice would you send back
to yourself from the future to ensure this best happens?' Their
advice: 'Stop procrastinating and go for it. Just do it. Believe in
yourself.' Such phrases could easily be titles of Eurovision entries.
You know the sort: 'Boom bang a bang live your dreams yey!' Their
advice is about the inner wisdom we all possess and which is the
path to fulfilling their own potential. Songs usually follow this pat-

tern, with verses about the obstacles in the way and a rousing chorus that is a simple call to action.

They involve groups

We can enjoy many things on our own, and sometimes we have no choice, but there are some things best done with at least one other person in the room. Passing on skills, advice and information can be equally effective to individuals or groups but inspiration is best delivered to a number of people. We're social animals. Why else would people go to Glastonbury when they could buy a CD and listen to the same songs in better sound quality and in dry surroundings? Or go to a football stadium or theatre when there are 50-inch plasma screens? It's because a powerful energy can be created and absorbed in a crowd that can inspire us to believe we are able to achieve more and think we might be better than we thought. As a teacher or trainer we can create and direct this energy like the conductor of a symphony orchestra.

They don't include the most important ingredient: your attitude

This has the biggest impact of all. If you're positive, curious and genuinely interested in the people out front, you should be fine. If you'd rather be somewhere else, then please go somewhere else. Change career – you and those around you deserve it. I attended a fascinating 10-day NLP trainer course a few years ago and a great deal of time was spent on this part of presenting. For more on this see *Presenting Magically* by Tad James and David Shephard.

Teenagers need adults to be their guide. In his book *Flow*, Mihaly Csikszentmihalyi suggests parents of happy children offer the following:

- Clarity – clear goals and feedback.
- Centring – a focus on the present, not harping on about past misdemeanours or future failures if you don't buck up your ideas etc.

- Choice – with stated consequences.
- Commitment – they trust their child and let them do their own thing.
- Challenge – they stretch the child.

These five themes offer everyone working with children a useful reminder of the right attitude to choose. As well as your attitude, consider your appearance. Young people say they respect teachers that are good looking and cool. OK, before you make a dash for your nearest cosmetic surgery clinic, try these two ideas first.

Clothes: don't wear anything older than the students you teach. You may be sentimentally attached to a pair of trousers you bought when Wham! were in their heyday, but just because you can still squeeze into them doesn't mean you have to.

Personal grooming: give it a go! If you smell, have stray hairs growing from places other than the top of your head, or have breath that can wilt roses, then don't look up your nickname on *Friends Reunited*.

If like me you used to turn heads but now you turn stomachs, worry not. Like the hooded top, wrinkles receive a bad press. Greet each new wrinkle as a monument to your burgeoning wisdom. And the most cost-effective treatment for wrinkles is a dimmer switch in the bedroom.

Students need to be able to respect and trust us as professional adults, not mock our ageing sadness – that's what they have parents for. Luckily, although students say they prefer good-looking and 'cool' teachers, the teachers they most respect are those that offer warmth, respect, firmness and knowledge of their subject. We can all work out to improve these factors without paying for gym membership or expensive suits ... though the suit will come in handy for parents' evenings.

I've shared many of the activities described in this book and it has been great to receive positive feedback from people working with some of the most challenging groups. I've never white water rafted or partaken in extreme ironing, but inspiring a year group of 150 teenagers must be every bit as exhilarating. I hope you find activities that inspire you and those around you. Is there anything better we can do?

And that brings us nicely back to my three pairs of pants for the larger lady activity, which I reproduce for you now in full, using the playing cards format. Give it a go. You know you want to ...

J
Big Pants
Time: 5–10 mins

Activity: Split the group into teams. Their challenge is to come up with as many incorrect wrong ways as possible to put on the pants. They demonstrate one and then pass the pants to the next person. The game is against the clock. They start when the music starts and stop when it stops. The game can be competitive in which the team with most variations wins, or collaborative, where you add all the scores together to reach 50.

Learning Point: We don't try stuff if we think we're going to look stupid. So some people never try anything, they never reach their potential. In most areas of life getting it wrong is not as bad as never trying anything. This attitude of 'feedback not failure' is central to success in life. The thought of doing things is often worse than the experience itself.

Preparation: You'll need a collection of big, oversized comedy pants and/or thongs, enough for one pair per six to eight people. You'll also need music. Comedy music like the theme to *Benny Hill* or other up-tempo songs are ideal.

J

PART ONE

PART ONE

Go For It

Believe in Yourself

Know Your Strengths

Have a Plan

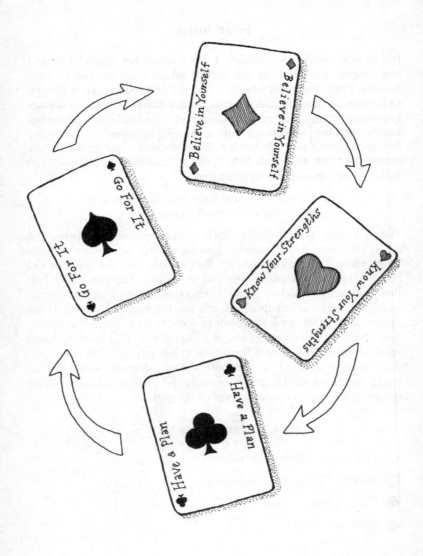

Four Suits

It's 25 years since I left school. I don't remember much of what I was taught, though I do get excited when I see an oxbow lake, because I can remember how it is formed and could draw it for you in a series of three neat diagrams. I can still remember how a large proportion of the teachers made me feel. The teachers I remember fondly are those who taught me to believe in myself, discover my strengths, find a path to develop those strengths and go for it. The activities in this book can help students remember the impact you had 25 years from now. In a nutshell:

> *Students don't care how much you know until they*
> *know how much you care.*

The four suits each represent a step within the process of being and doing our best. I read recently about the next generation of computer games. It sounds amazing, they'll make the Wii seem as old fashioned as the computer tennis of the 1980s. There will be a helmet with sensors locked on to areas of our brain that are able to respond directly to our thoughts and put them on the screen. Think 'spider' and it will appear in front of you. At least, that's the prediction. Perhaps we're getting ahead of ourselves. This book is based on the idea that we should learn how to interact with the real world first. Most of us don't interact with the world nearly as well as we could do. Think of the four steps outlined here as a kind of dress rehearsal for the computer games of the future.

Four Suits

◆ Diamonds – Believe in Yourself

♥ Hearts – Know Your Strengths

♣ Clubs – Have a Plan

♠ Spades – Go For It

And one last thought for your journey through my exercises: a life based on doing and being is more fulfilling than a life based on having. Remember, the best way to inspire others to be their best is for us to be *our* best. I have always had an ambition to have a book published. When it happened, my children told me they were proud of me. Better still, my daughter said *she* would write a book when she was older.

'No offence Dad, but it will be better than yours,' she said.

Wow: just by observing me achieve my dreams she was growing bigger dreams for herself.

THE ACTIVITIES

Joker: Body Parts

Jokers are a great place to start. Jokers appear in many cultures as tricksters, clowns or magicians. There are 'magic' tricks at the end of this book but we'll start with two activities that whenever I've used them ensured that a session got off to a great start. Laughter is the safe release of nervous energy and tension. Laughter in groups is special because it brings us all together in the present, alert and ready to be taken on a journey. When we laugh we feel like we're playing, and when we play we really learn. Purposeful play is as powerful in the classroom as it is outside. In *The Fish Philosophy*, Luden, Paul and Christensen describe the positive impact a playful attitude can have within organisations. When people adopt a positive playful attitude even potentially negative working environments, such as a smelly fish market, can be enjoyable spaces.

While setting up this element of a task some members of the group, usually the boys, will be thinking of a rude answer. I sometimes try and pre-empt this if I think there's a danger that some will not be careful over their choice of words. Not everyone will shout out a body part but those that do will usually provide you with an accurate idea of just how energised the group is for your session. If you hear replies above waist high you're doing well.

A longer version of this activity asks for three scores out of 10 for Energy, Openness and Focus. It's useful for adult groups and is described in full by Dave Keeling in *The Big Book of Independent Thinking*. High scores relate to flow and memorable experiences – when we're at our best. We remember vividly the times we reach 10, 10, 10. These are the best moments of our lives. How many do most people achieve? A dozen? How many have you achieved so far? How many more are you going to have? Why not go for more, what harm could it do to raise your game and aim for more golden moments? Go on, check your diary for this weekend! Curiously, three 10s can also explain how many a phobia is burned-in to the wiring of the brain. But more on that later ...

J

Body Parts
Time: 2–3 mins

Activity: Say, 'I'm going to do my best to provide a brilliant session. I'm full of energy and enthusiasm. I need to know how much energy and enthusiasm you have as a group. In a moment I'm going to ask you to shout out a body part based on how you're feeling now. If you've got loads of energy, enthusiasm, and are going to make the most of this session, shout out a body part from the neck upwards. If you can hardly be bothered to answer then that would be from the ankle or below.'

You then say, '1, 2, 3', and you'll have an idea of how focused your group is on your session.

Learning Point: Your attitude has the biggest influence on your success, more so than exam results or anything else. If you are not in a positive, relaxed, focused mood you will not be able to do anywhere near your best.

Preparation: None.

J

Joker: Tongue Twister

This is a natural follow-up to the body parts activity. A great way to increase the energy in a room is to have fun with someone else, and tongue twisters are a quick way to achieve this. Tongue twisters are routinely used by speech therapists to help recovering stroke patients improve their speech. They develop concentration and links between important parts of the brain, and are surely more fun than Sudoku!

Most people, if they follow your instructions, will swear while saying this tongue twister. Then they'll laugh, usually quite loudly.

When they've finished you can remind the group that the energy level has risen. You can ask how many managed to say the rhyme five times without making a mistake, and praise with congratulations. Offer a swear box to the rest.

There are many other tongue twisters you could try. I like this one because it's a little bit naughty. It once kept my children howling with laughter for a 20-minute car journey, which is not to be sniffed at.

After this activity you've raised the energy and sense of anticipation in the group and they're now ready for you to work your teachery magic.

J

Tongue Twister
Time: 2–3 mins

Activity: Tell the group you are going to give them a tongue twister and, working in pairs, they have to say it to each other, fast, five times without making a mistake.

When everyone is quiet say:

• Who shot the city sheriff?

Alternative tongue twisters include:

• Three free throws, Cheap ship trip.
• Black bug's blood, Peggy Babcock.

Learning Point: The energy in the room will increase when there is laughter and people engage with each other. We can learn to use this energy or state to help us learn more effectively.

Preparation: None.

J

21

DIAMONDS

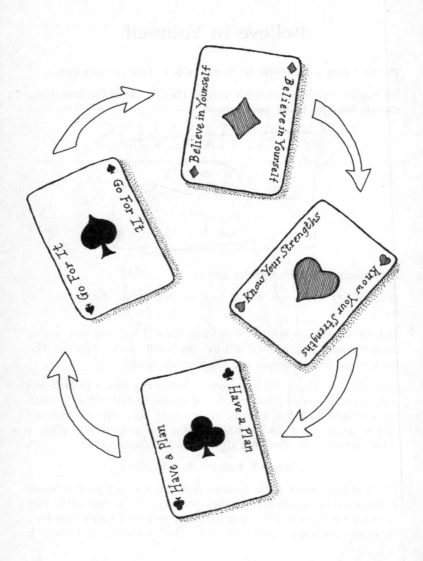

Believe in Yourself

The first step to believing in ourselves is to take compliments.

We're great at this when we're young. This picture is the first thing my son brought home from school.

He brought it home when he was 13.

Only joking – he was about four or five. What did we say to him?

Did we say, 'That's brilliant that, well done, I love the way you've done the body, etc, etc.' Or did we say, 'Well, that's crap that! The body is out of proportion and the legs are wrong.'

Obviously we chose the first option. We pretty much praised our son non-stop while he was small. The result: he believed in himself. Little people have big dreams. He thought he could do anything and be anyone. For a while his ambition was to be a Jedi. What a great ambition, to travel the Universe with a light sabre!

Praise = Belief = Big dreams

Children take praise for a specific skill and also accept it to mean praise for their whole person, their identity. This is fine while they are young but potentially dangerous for teenagers because they hear far more criticism of their (lack of) skills from adults and peers. If this is 'generalised' to form part of their sense of identity, then 'I'm in the lower maths group' can end up leading to 'so I must be thick and useless as a person.' The intention may be to help children form a realistic idea of their strengths and skills, ('I'm only telling you you're useless for your own good') but the danger of this generalising process – when a lack of skill in one area can lead to a belief we're a useless person – is ominous indeed. For more on this see the *Star Sign* activity.

Ask a group of adults how many of them hear a little voice in their heads saying, 'You're useless and the world is going to find out' just before important events like dates, job interviews or presentations. Chances are all of them will respond with a nervous laugh and admission of guilt. There is evidence of this pattern all around us in schools, and young people – and adults – deserve better than this.

Sometimes the reverse happens. Contestants on grotesque TV programmes use their sense of identity and skill to convince themselves they are the next Leona Lewis or Paul Potts because they think 'I'm a great person and want to be a singer therefore I'm a great singer.' This is the equivalent of wanting to be a Jedi when you're 40. It's cute when you're eight but slightly embarrassing when you're an adult with a receding hairline and beer belly. I apologise to the thousands of adult *Star Wars* fans out there, especially the female ones with receding hairlines and beer bellies; life can seem unnecessarily cruel at times.

From time to time I ask groups, 'How many of you broke an arm or leg when you were young?' Some of the ones who did will want to share gruesome details with the group. I then ask those who haven't broken an arm or leg, 'How many of you secretly were hoping you'd break a bone for the extra attention and popularity?' It's amazing that most say 'yes' with alacrity. Well, it's not really amazing because we all miss the undivided and positive attention we received as babies and toddlers.

Diamonds - Believe in Yourself

So how can we become confident, self-aware adults with a realistic and accurate sense of our strengths and areas of weaknesses? The solution is to be offered – and learn how to accept – specific and evidence-based praise for **what** we do well to help us to discover **what** we're good at doing. We can then learn to accept praise without feeling we're being arrogant and accept feedback – not criticism – without doubting our self worth, our sense of **who** we are.

Ace of Diamonds: Compliments Slip

The *Compliments Slip* activity is both the start and heart of this process. We need to accept feedback on what we do and evaluate it to build the picture of who we are, without thinking it *is* the picture of who we are. A note of caution here: when you ask teenagers to compliment each other they may be reluctant or slightly embarrassed, especially boys. This proves the point! Once boys do praise each other, it can bring a tear to the eye. One lad said to a friend, 'Well, I suppose you're quite funny.' His friend beamed and gleamed, 'So you're saying I've got a good sense of humour, cool.' I know this is unfamiliar territory for most British people; we'd rather chew off our own hand than accept praise, but it is crucial to our growth.

When Kenneth Brannagh, interviewed by Andrew Marr, was reminded that he never read reviews until the end of a play's run, he replied, 'Oh yes, I think you should score your own card.' The wisdom in his approach is twofold: first, assess ourselves (know your strengths); second, listen to feedback to help you to become better, but not to the extent it stops you from going for it.

One final point: I read a survey that suggested 36% of British teenagers would not consider self-employment for fear of failure, compared to 18% in the United States. This is a big difference and something we need to address. This activity is a start.

A   Compliments Slip
Time: 5 mins

Activity: Tell the group that part of believing in ourselves is to be able to accept compliments. Say, 'I'd like you to turn to the person you're sitting next to and compliment them. It has to be something positive you believe to be true about the person. It could be about their personality (funny, warm ...), a skill they have (good at football, music ...) or physical (they have nice hair ...).' They swap compliments with each other and they have to just enjoy it and then say, 'Thank you.'

Learning Point: It has been said that, for every compliment a teenager is given, they receive nine negative comments from teachers, parents and peers. This will generally lead to them feeling bad about themselves and even stop them from believing the compliments they receive.

Preparation: None.

A

2 of Diamonds: Inside Out

If you don't create your reality your reality will create you.

Lizzie West, songwriter

So, being good or bad at something, such as having a skill, doesn't mean you're a good or bad person i.e. your identity. We often forget this. *Inside Out* explores this idea.

After the activity, most people notice that they take in any negative stuff directed at them, but don't accept the positive. They can see how this will lead to a negative self image and identity.

For example, if someone says you look nice, you might think they don't really mean it, or assume that it's the top you're wearing that's nice, rather than yourself. Whereas, if someone says you look awful, you might believe it and feel bad, telling yourself, 'Oh yes, I'm awful, me!' as you run through in your head all the things you think *are* awful about you.

The opposite way, taking in only positives and ignoring negatives, can make us deluded. Watch the early rounds of *Britain's Got Talent* or *The X Factor* and we see people who genuinely believe they're top singers belting out *My Heart Will Go On* whilst you wish for the exact opposite to be true.

When actress Teri Hatcher was asked why she called her autobiography *Burnt Toast* she said it was because it spoke volumes about her mother's self-worth. While making breakfast toast, if her mum burnt a slice, she wouldn't give it to daughter or put it in the bin, she'd take it for herself. Teri Hatcher recognised the danger of passing on to your children this message about the lack of self-belief. She vowed to break the cycle with her own child. Our attitude towards ourselves will pass on as powerful a message to those we are with as our attitude towards them.

2

Inside Out
Time: 5-6 mins

Activity: Ask the group to stand up.

Say 'I'm going to give you two options and I'd like you to stand or sit down depending upon which one suits you better. OK? I'd like you to stay standing if you ignore negative stuff said to you (it bounces off) or sit down if you accept it (take it inside).'

Next, repeat the activity but this time for positive stuff. Do they let it bounce off (stand) or take it inside (sit down)?

Learning Point: Discuss the impact for those who stand and those who sit: if you stand both times that's good, if you sit both times that's bad! We need to learn to think of things others say to us as feedback not criticism.

Preparation: None.

2

3 of Diamonds: Parachute Jump

People often stop trying because they think they'll be wrong. They believe that doing something wrong – a skill or lack of it – means they're a bad person in their identity. When we do things wrong we feel bad, so to stop feeling bad we'll not try to do things. This means we risk not learning about ourselves and may never discover our strengths.

Being wrong can only happen if we're asked questions that only have one correct answer. Most questions, or tasks and challenges as they are presented in work and life outside of education, have more than one answer. Even questions with one answer can have different paths to the same answer.

The *Parachute Jump* question gives people the chance to think of loads of possible answers – some funny (landing in a pillow or mattress factory), some ingenious (landing on a giant spring, jumping from a small height) and some a glimpse into the workings of a male teenage brain (landing on Jordan's breast implants).

Statistically, survival rates are highest when people land in soft snow or trees (although, as one teenager pointed out, probably not on top of a Christmas tree). Landing in water is a popular choice but I'm told this is bad, as at high speeds it is the same as landing on concrete.

This activity goes really well with *Three of Hearts: Spelling Strategy*.

'Reframing' is used in NLP to help people change their perspective. Seeing things in a different way helps us generate new ideas and beliefs and offers us more choice and therefore control. Not a bad habit to develop. Ian Gilbert's *The Little Book of Thunks* series of books develop this habit. Questions can be helpful, particularly if it prevents us from inadvertently destroying the self-belief and entrepreneurial spirit we so need to see flourish in our young people. Reframing is a really useful way to find a positive meaning from seemingly negative experiences. Inventors often say their experiments haven't failed, they've just ruled out another way not to achieve the desired outcome. They do not give up. The story of Pollyanna is a good example of reframing in action. Think of reframing as providing a parachute to help someone waft gently to a soft and safe landing, rather than sharply on to the point of a spiky Christmas tree.

3 Parachute Jump
Time: 5 mins

Activity: Challenge the group to think of as many ways you could survive a parachute jump if the parachute didn't open. A clue, if needed, is landing in something soft. Teams work best with this activity, as more ideas are usually generated than working individually.

Learning Point: We can all think creatively and come up with answers to most questions. Most of the challenges we face in life don't just have one best solution or answer; there are many. In school the emphasis is on right and wrong.

Preparation: None.

4 of Diamonds: Paper Wait

'Wrong' and 'right' are interesting concepts.

The *Paper Wait* activity illustrates the value of letting people find the answer themselves safely and without fear of ridicule. This is particularly important when what they're exploring is themselves.

I've suggested to some groups that this activity uses the scientific method:

1. Have a thought.

2. Make a prediction (guess).

3. Test it enough times for a rule or answer to emerge.

4. Then, and only then, know something new or interesting.

Science teacher colleagues may challenge you on this, as there is discussion amongst scientists about whether or not it is a valid scientific method. I'm happy to leave that discussion to scientists. In a way it highlights the shades of grey (or the rainbow of colours) between black and white. On the other hand, some youngsters have told me it's the first science lesson they've enjoyed.

In his book *Out of Our Minds*, Sir Ken Robinson, a brilliant speaker and author on creativity, describes four stages to creativity: preparation, incubation, illumination and verification. Basically, creativity is a process not an event. We need to help everyone, especially teenagers, build self-awareness and self-belief in this way. Life, not just creativity, is best experienced like this rather than as a series of metaphorical punches to the head as we absorb more and more information about things we can't do.

I remember at school playing along with the game. Learning nine functions of the liver for Biology GCSE, I said to my teacher, 'This is boring! When can we start learning instead of regurgitating bits of irrelevant information?' I figured my liver already knew. She said I'd have to wait until A level. One year later I reminded her of our conversation when she told us we'd need to remember 15 functions of the liver. 'Wait until University,' she replied. She must have loved teaching me! As an undergraduate I was told to wait until Post Graduate and my enthusiasm vanished. At least I'd lasted until I was 20. Too many lose interest in education before they're even teenagers. Should we be in our twenties before we start learning?

In his book *The Hungry Spirit*, Charles Handy outlines his ingredients for a successful education system in the modern world:

- The discovery of oneself is more important than the discovery of the world.

- Everyone is good at something.

- Life is a marathon not a horse race (don't focus on regular tests at 7, 11, 14 to the exclusion of co-operation, team working, curiosity and confidence).

- The best learning happens after doing/developing opportunities for reflective learning rather than so much content (most education comes before experience).

To me Charles Handy makes a lot of sense. Time for a paradigm shift?

I'm often invited to work in organisations to improve communication skills, help individuals cope with change and develop leadership qualities. These subjects are explored in many books covering acres of shelf space in bookshops across the country. One of the best is *Who Moved My Cheese?* by Dr Spencer Johnson. His book extols the value of being able to anticipate change, adapt to and enjoy change and be ready to change quickly, again and again. The mindset of people able to do this is not fostered by the GCSE/ 'A' Level exam production line our education system is built upon.

In his book *What's The Point of School?*, Guy Claxton highlights the qualities of confident learners. They are:

- curious;

- courageous;
- able to explore and investigate;
- imaginative;
- able to reason/analyse/evaluate;
- sociable; and
- flexible.

Claxton offers an alternative to 'Get on with your work.'

The following questions will develop the qualities he champions:

'How are you going to go about that?'

'What is hard about that?'

'How else could you do that?'

'What could you do to help yourself if you get stuck?'

'How could you help someone else do that?'

Diamonds – Believe in Yourself

4

Paper Wait
Time: 5-10 mins

Activity: Ask the group to predict how many times they can fold a piece of A4 paper in half.

Ask for suggestions from the group and note the lowest and highest predictions offered, usually 4 to 10.

Then each person folds until they arrive at an answer, 6. And they all do! Some boys will usually insist they can achieve 7.

Learning Point: They're all right in the end. Being right at the beginning is not important, reaching an answer is the purpose of most activities.

Preparation: You'll need one sheet of A4 paper per person.

4

5 of Diamonds: Body Talk

Body balancing illustrates in a physical way the concept that we are stronger, better directed and more focused when we're relaxed and thinking of the task in hand rather than when we are tense or angry. We should focus on the learning, and not on whether we'll look stupid, otherwise we'll try less and learn less. Sometimes, less is not more. Group members good at performing in sport, drama, dance or music will confirm this. Superficially, anger can appear to give us strength and determination but it blurs and distorts real strength. Peak performance results from a relaxed strength, sometimes referred to as 'flow' – being present and 'in the zone'. To believe in ourselves we need to be relaxed, calm and feel in control.

In her book *The Secrets of the Teenage Brain*, Sheryl Feinstein identifies sources of stress for teenagers: exams; appearance; peer comments/ relationships; unrealistic classroom demands; the future; and disagreements with significant people. Many of the strategies suggested to overcome these stressors are mirrored in the activities contained within this book. Teenagers do not have to feel bad about themselves. This activity shows them how they can recognise their moods and choose ones that help them achieve their goals.

5

Body Talk
Time: 5-8 mins

Activity: We're going to explore real strength.

Ask for a volunteer and get them to stand on one leg and make their body stiff, as if they were angry. You then demonstrate how you can easily push them off balance. Then you ask them to balance on one leg (like Daniel from *Karate Kid* in 'crane' position) while feeling relaxed and thinking about being strong. You push and they'll be stronger this time. You can then ask the group to try this in pairs.

Learning Point: We are at our best when relaxed and focused.

When we're angry or nervous we will not be strong.

We make better decisions when we're relaxed and focused. Many people make big decisions when they're angry.

Preparation: None.

5

6 of Diamonds: Group Challenge

This is an energiser activity similar to *Parachute Jump*.

Assess the group, or ask, to determine whether they wish to work co-operatively or competitively. Each team adds their scores together to see if they can beat the best-ever total (currently 75) or work in tables against each other. Generally, boys like to be competitive and girls co-operative. I don't mind as long as they play.

Other examples include giving different tables different objects and asking them to come up with as many uses as possible for the object. You can bring in things from home. If you're a Primary school teacher it seems to be a compulsion to collect items from your house and neighbourhood and take them to school. I wonder sometimes what it must be like living with a Primary teacher. Things must regularly go missing and end up in classrooms. Actually, it must be like living with me, as I take all sorts with me to my training sessions including rubber gloves, big knickers (see earlier), water pistols, umbrellas and Russian dolls.

I was stopped at Customs once when flying to a venue and had to open my case and talk a bemused security official through a bizarre collection of items. He seemed very interested and thankfully decided against any deeper probing than trying on one of the glove puppets I had with me. Though I'm told there are worse gloves a customs officer can put on ...

6

Group Challenge
Time: 10 mins

Activity: Each group is seated around a table and given three to five objects. They have to think of as many uses as possible for each object within a time limit, five minutes is good.

Learning Point: This activity encourages divergent thinking and creativity.

The purpose of these activities can also be to highlight that creativity is fun and we can all do it. Our brains work better when they're allowed to be creative and RING (are Relevant, Interesting, Naughty or a Giggle). We can believe in ourselves because we all have this amazing brain.

Preparation: You will need some objects.

Sometimes I just improvise with stuff in the room I'm in but if you add in some unusual items it enhances the activity. A rubber glove, fluffy toy, leaf, etc. results in more creativity and fun.

6

7 of Diamonds: Animal Impression

I sometimes wonder how I ever get away with this activity – groups of cool teenagers enthusiastically impersonating a gorilla, sheep or tiger and laughing with their friends. It may be because I use this part of the way through a session, when they're warmed up and 'with' me. Tips to enhance your success rate include splitting the group into two to compete against each other, especially good during the pantomime season, and playing upbeat music during the impressions.

There have been a few occasions when this hasn't worked, but when it does it illustrates one of the key reasons why some people are successful in life and others are not so fortunate. And it's worth the risk. If it doesn't work I move on to another activity from this section or ask, 'Why do you think we learn best when we're young before we get to school?' After hearing the answers from the group, usually in line with my answer I say, 'It's because we don't get embarrassed. If we want to know what it's like to be a tiger we get down on all fours and start roaring.' Young children laugh and cry up to 200 times a day; most adults don't manage that many in a month.

Those that join in with this activity are demonstrating the great quality of thinking like young children. Einstein said he tried to be child-like but not childish. I congratulate and thank those that take part with enthusiasm, as this attitude will probably have a bigger impact on how successful someone is in life than anything else, including qualifications and attractiveness; although they also help.

Richard Branson bravely admitted in an interview a few years ago that for a long time he didn't know the difference between gross and net profit. Such honesty is a characteristic of many successful people. When someone admits they don't know everything we trust and like them more than people who pretend to know all of the answers. This honesty also reveals Richard Branson as a lifelong learner – a great attitude to nurture in all students.

7

Animal Impression
Time: 3-10 mins

Activity: Share with the group the research that suggests people prepared to look silly usually achieve more in life.

Offer to give the group a chance to find out.

Say you will reveal an animal to your half of the group and they have to impersonate it to see if the other half can guess what it is. Then repeat in reverse with another animal. Say, I bet those who join in have a good time, a laugh, and those who don't join in will feel embarrassed – not the other way round. If it goes well, have more than one round.

Good luck. When it works, it's a brilliant activity.

Learning Point: We learn more when we are prepared to try stuff without worrying about how we may appear. That's why young children learn so well. If you ask a four-year-old what it's like to be a tiger they'll get down on the floor and start roaring at you.

Preparation: You'll either need a few soft toys or glove puppets, or you could use drawings of the animals. In my experience the best animals are gorilla, sheep, lion, snake, horse/donkey, fish, and T-Rex. If you want to be sneaky, put in a few silent animals.

7

8 of Diamonds: First Date

Ask your group to think about how they'd behave on a first date with someone they really, really fancied. They could draw a little version of themselves on a sheet of A4 and write their thoughts around it. (Alternatively they could work on a group answer, or discuss and provide feedback after a suitable time.) Common responses are 'polite', 'washed', 'smart', 'funny', 'happy', 'cool', and 'nervous'. One lad recently said he'd even pretend to be interested in what the girl was saying! I do hope he finds a partner he really does find interesting. Ask everyone to swap sheets and 'rate their date' out of 10, based on the words they've written, then return to originator. They can repeat the activity on the other side of the sheet, describing themselves at their worst – perhaps with parents or in a lesson they dislike.

Ask the group, 'Which is the real you? How often are you at your best? What could you achieve at your best?' The more time we spend behaving towards people, including to ourselves, like we do when we're on a first date, the better results we'll achieve.

I suggest that if they ask their mum what their dad was like on their first Saturday together, she wouldn't say he lay on the sofa in his pants watching *Sky Sports News*. He'd have been out shopping with her, smiling as she tried on loads of outfits saying encouraging things such as, 'That looks brilliant!' while *thinking* about lying on the sofa watching *Sky Sports News* in his pants.

This links well with *Ace of Clubs*, when students have rated themselves at less than 100%, because it proves we can up our game.

The same thing applies in work situations. People start by getting in early and staying late to finish off projects, and their faces can hurt with all the concerted smiling at anyone passing in the corridors. Then, after three months they're farting at the photocopier and eating crisps over the keyboard. Actually, I've never eaten crisps over a keyboard.

8

First Date
Time: 10 mins

Activity: Ask the group to think about how they'd behave, and strive to be at their best, on a first date with someone they really, really fancied. *Washed* is the most common answer from boys, with *new clothes and hairstyle* featuring for girls.

Discuss with the group: Which is the real you? How often are you at your best? When will you raise your game (job interviews, sport)?

Learning Point: Behaving towards people in the way we do when we're on a first date will bring us more success in life. We *can* raise our game. Successful people are those raising their game for longer in order to achieve goals that are important to them.

Preparation: Sheets of paper and pens (optional).

8

9 of Diamonds: Speed Dating

To believe in yourself you need to share information about yourself, to give and receive feedback so you can build an accurate picture of your real strengths. It can also start the process of networking. One of the things successful people have in common is the willingness to enthusiastically share information and ideas about their aims and ideas. The people we talk to can then often offer information or advice, or suggest we contact someone they know who could help us.

In most epic stories the hero is offered advice and support by a guide or sage. These are traditionally tribal elders or parent/grandparent figures. We can all benefit from the additional support available. It is widely stated that we know someone who knows someone who knows David Beckham (or anyone else, for that matter). This activity is a simple example of sharing information and we soon find out the things we have in common – or not – with others.

Young children are naturally gifted at this. If they don't know how a toy works they shove it in front of an adult for a demonstration; if the adult can't help they'll take it to another adult because children are natural networkers.

9

Speed Dating
Time: 10–15 mins

Activity: Run a mock speed dating session in the group. Use a musical chairs approach so that each person talks to at least four other people. This works best when done quickly. Don't give people time to think themselves out of joining in. Give a question with a strict time limit (20 seconds per person). Questions could include:

- Which famous person would you most like to be or meet and why?
- What are you most scared of?
- What's your most and least favourite food?
- Which is your favourite TV show?
- If you could have one wish what would it be?
- How would you spend a million pounds in a week?

Reveal questions one at a time to add to the element of excitement and surprise.

Learning Point: To believe in ourselves we need to talk to people, take interest in others and find out about ourselves. Networking is one of the main ways people find jobs and receive useful information about what is going on.

Preparation: None.

9

10 of Diamonds: Line Up

This is a useful way to start a session. I use many different questions, here are two of the best:

'Line up in order of the date you were born, January this end (left) through to December the other end (right), and talk to the person you're standing next to. Describe the best and worst birthday/ Christmas presents you've received.'

The purpose of the activity is to encourage people to talk to each other. This is the way we receive feedback that can help us develop our self-awareness.

An alternative is to ask people to line up based on the distance they live from the school/college. Ask them to share something they like about their environment (bedroom, house, garden, close friends). The learning point in this question is that our environment plays a crucial role in our life chances. Certain post codes are considered good or bad. Students can be encouraged not to let such external factors act as barriers to their own success. The character Frank Costello, played by Jack Nicholson, in *The Departed* says,

> *I don't want to be a product of my environment.*
> *I want my environment to be a product of me.*

Wow, what an attitude that is surely worth nurturing.

When the singer Natasha Bedingfield was asked what is the best advice she has been given, she replied,

> *To remember I'm in the driving seat, in whatever direction my career*
> *goes, never be a victim, I'm always in control.*

Go girl.

10

Line up
Time: 5 mins

Activity: Ask the group to line up based on:

• the month in which they were born, or

• the distance they live from the school or college.

Then ask them to share information – best/worst birthday presents or something they like about where they live. Ask some to share their answers with the group.

Learning Point: For the month you were born option: talking to people is a great way to develop our self-awareness.

For the distance traveled to the school/college the learning point is that environment can have a major impact on our life chances. Compare the life chances of someone born in Africa and Europe. Certain housing estates or districts can have a reputation as good or bad places to live. I attempt to deal with this potentially sensitive subject by asking the opinion of the group and then stressing the possibility of each person taking control of their own destiny and not looking for reasons to explain future failure.

Preparation: None.

10

Jack of Diamonds: Lie Detector

Ask a volunteer to stand in front of you and raise an arm. They then say out loud something they believe to be true five times, and on the third or fourth repetition you press down on their wrist to check resistance. They rest, then repeat with a statement they believe not to be true, and on the third or fourth you check resistance. People are nearly always stronger the first time. This is because we're stronger when we're being true to ourselves.

The group can try out the experiment in pairs. Remember, these games are metaphors; we generally know whether the activities we're engaged in are going to be good or bad for us. We can develop our self-awareness and learn to tap into our inner wisdom far more than we do. This is not meant to replace logic and reasoning skills, but intuition can bring a great deal to the decision-making process. That's why people often say, 'I'll sleep on it' before making big decisions. It often helps us work through an issue intuitively. Ask teenagers hypothetical questions and test their reactions, either with the arm push or allow them to process the question internally; they are usually surprised at the accuracy of their gut reaction. Sample questions/statements could include:

Taking drugs is good; I'm making the most of my skills and talents; I eat a healthy diet.

I provide very safe examples of statements to use on the card opposite and these are enough for most sessions, but it is possible to explore a wide range of issues with this activity. NLP uses this kind of process to help people discover strength, belief and choice from within, rather than imposing it externally.

Sometimes this activity does not work, because people know what is supposed to happen and consciously make the opposite take place. I don't mind this because it works the majority of the time. If some people prefer scepticism, fine, as long as it is not used as a shield to protect them from new ideas.

J

Lie Detector
Time: 5-10 mins

Activity: Ask for a volunteer or two – to encourage a quicker response.

I usually use two, as they share the spotlight and any perceived risk/embarrassment, and it also gives any activity two chances to work. Ask the volunteer to stretch out an arm (mummy/sleep walking style) and ask them to repeat their name five times. On the third or fourth, press down on their wrist to check resistance/strength. Repeat with the person giving a false name (such as 'My name is Victoria Beckham', if it's a male volunteer) five times and check resistance again. They are nearly always stronger when telling the truth.

Repeat with the second volunteer, using a statement they believe to be true ('I believe I'm good at drama', 'Sunderland are the best team in the North East') five times followed by a statement they believe is not true.

Ask the group to follow the activity in pairs.

Learning Point: We're stronger when being true to our beliefs and strengths.

Preparation: None.

J

Queen of Diamonds: Mind Power

This activity takes a few minutes to set up. It is remarkably popular; it demonstrates the power within.

The activity is enjoyed by adults as well as teenagers and you will usually win over any doubters because it works for the majority of the group. Many people are quite excited and genuinely pleased with themselves after this activity. Once everyone has had a go it's best to move on quickly to minimise the chances of the materials being used as improvised weapons! I collect in the materials afterwards, so I'm not causing problems for the next teacher working with the group.

This activity is based on the idea that wisdom is not only in our heads, it is in our body too. We feel as well as think. Before your inner, beardy intellectual jumps on your shoulder and starts to tut disapprovingly, worry not, I merely advocate we use both rather than only one. Both are good. Hey, there's a place for an inner hippy in a hemp smock too. That's why we have two shoulders. If you don't believe me, sleep on it. Our mind and body are linked; they are not two distinct systems. They influence each other. Western cultures tend to separate the two. Eastern cultures tend to explore and develop both together, for example, through meditation. The amazing interplay between both systems is described beautifully by Candace Pert in her book *Molecules of Emotion*. She describes her successful search to find endorphins, the body's natural happy chemicals, and understand their role in mind–body processes.

The moods we feel have a big impact on our performance. More on this later, for now, enjoy the activity.

Q

Mind Power
Time: 10 mins

Activity: Take a 10cm piece of thread and stick a pea-size ball of Blu-Tack to the end (processed pea size, not marrowfat or petit pois; someone always asks). It should look like a conker.

Give the full instructions before they start.

Say you will hold the string and rest the Blu-Tack on the palm of your other hand. You will then decide which way it will swing; it can either go side to side in a straight line or round in a circle before you lift it about 3cm from your palm. It will move the way you think it will without you consciously or deliberately moving it. Try it a few times, changing the direction you think it will go.

It works for 95% of people every time they try it.

Learning Point: We have more power, ability, control and potential than we think we have.

Preparation: You will need a reel of cotton thread and Blu-Tack.

Q

King of Diamonds: Memory Lane/I Believe

Thinking of times we were at our best can be powerful. Remembering in detail what we could see, hear and feel accesses empowering states. It is worth reinforcing good habits. Teenagers often struggle to think of times they were great. An exception is sporting success. I ask them to share a really funny time or experience with their partner, a story that will have you crying with laughter. When teenagers do share such stories it is heart warming. I often work with teenagers having a bad time at school and/or home. Hearing them laugh their heads off is great. We need to remember and relive these times. In smaller groups some are usually prepared to share their stories, which can lift the whole mood in the room. You this can help things along by sharing some of your own. If this is too much self-disclosure for you, *King of Spades* is an alternative activity.

The second part of this activity replicates how we create the experience of what is often labeled 'self-esteem'. Here, self-esteem refers to what we think of when we think of ourselves.

When someone is asked to think about themselves, they normally create a little montage in their head of a few experiences that leads to a specific feeling. For example, if I ask people to rate their self-esteem out of ten and I ask someone with a high score what happens in their head, the common response is as follows. They select from all of their memories three positive experiences, such as a time they were complimented by a parent, teacher, partner, a time they were good at a skill such as football, drama. These happen very quickly in the form of pictures/movie clips, self-talk and end in a good feeling which they translate to a default score. People with low self-esteem/worth follow the same path but in a negative direction, pulling out of their memories examples of them at their worst. Many hear teachers saying awful things about them. Don't ask anyone to share how they experience low self-esteem in a group. Only use positive experiences to explore boosting their own self-esteem. So you could ask someone who has high self-esteem and share it in a group but not someone with low self-esteem. This is an example of modelling and it is much used in NLP to help us understand how successful people think and behave.

I asked a group of adults to think about a time they felt brilliant. They could all think of an example, apart from one woman sitting at the front. To make her feel included I thought I'd encourage her and invited her to think of a time she felt wonderful. So she thought for a while and a little smile burst on to her face. 'Great. When was it?' I said helpfully. '1973,' she replied. I don't know about you, but I don't think that's often enough. Feeling great once every 35 years! Ten times a day is more like it.

This activity makes people feel good about themselves. You may start a habit.

The more schools can mimic the way people learn in real life the more they will build the self-belief of young people.

In Guy Claxton's *What's The Point of School?*, he offers observations regarding real life learning, suggesting that people:

- watch how other people do things and consider adapting it to suit their own style.
- go off by themselves and 'practise' the hard parts.
- ask their own questions, at their rate, and select their own 'teachers'.
- imagine and try out solutions to problems that are not finished, polished theories.
- reject some of their own ideas and adapt others.
- future-pace (imagine themselves doing something well as a home-movie in their heads).

The early developers of NLP used this approach to 'model' success-ful people. To find out how to overcome phobias Richard Bandler studied people who had overcome phobias and he created The Fast

Phobia Cure. I have used this approach to help many people overcome phobias myself.

Robert Dilts was interested in creativity so he studied Walt Disney and developed the Disney Creativity Strategy. I have used this approach with teams and witnessed an increase in the quality and quantity of creative ideas produced in a short space of time.

K

Memory Lane/I Believe
Time: 5–10 mins

Activity: (1) Memory Lane

Ask students, in pairs or group of three, to recount a funny story that had them laughing their heads off. What's the funniest thing that's ever happened to you? Invite someone to share their stories with the group.

(2) I Believe

Ask students to think of three times they felt great about themselves (maybe a rollercoaster ride, sporting success, family event, learning to do something well ...). Some will struggle to think of three so pester them. Ask them to link all three memories (see *Queen of Spades*). Perhaps they can add in a favourite up-beat song at full blast in their heads.

Learning Point: These activities put the person in a positive mood and then add on 'proof' that they're good at some things. This replicates how self-esteem happens in our heads.

Preparation: None.

K

HEARTS

Know Your Strengths

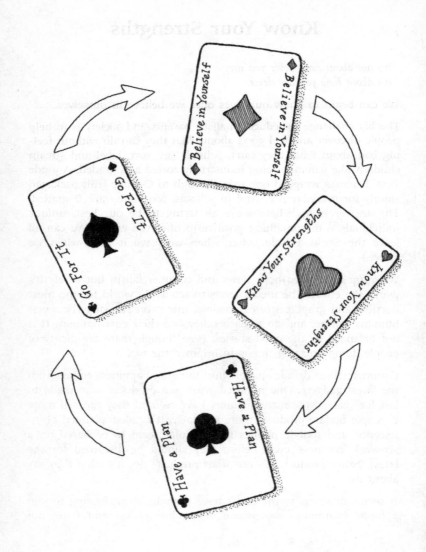

Know Your Strengths

It's not about how clever you are;
It's about how you are clever.

We can begin to know ourselves once we believe in ourselves.

The big challenge for educationalists, parents and society is to help people discover and feel good about what they can do without feeling bad about what they can't. Schools sift, sort, label and stream children like bananas being industrially sorted and graded. A-grade 'best' bananas wrapped one way, through to C-grade fruit packaged simply for everyday use. And in schools, too, many are D-graded. The answer is to believe we're all trying to be our best, unique individuals with something positive to offer the world. We can all leave the world a little better when we leave it than when we arrived.

We're up against 24-hour news and commercialism but surely it's worth the effort. The media tends to scour the world for the most horrible and graphic stories possible, intent on showing the worst humans can be, and do to each other and their environment. It is not balanced by the good stories, even though there are plenty of people doing amazing things to improve the world.

Commercialism deludes people into thinking happiness comes from the latest gadgets. One hundred years ago products were made to last for years. Now manufacturers have realised they can sell more if people update products more regularly. It's called 'planned obsolescence' and mobile phones in particular seem to be based on a six-week 'coolness' cycle before they should be discarded for the latest, better product. It's not what products do, it's what they say about us.

It seems madness to me and I have thought about leaving to join a hippy commune, somewhere my mobile phone and I are not ridiculed for being 'so last month'. Alas, I've never looked good in oversized rainbow coloured knitwear so here I stay.

The activities in this section are designed to help individuals discover their natural strengths, positively. As my dad said: 'Remember, you're better than nobody else but nobody else is better than you'. He also told me 'red sky at night shepherds' delight, red sky in the morning sailors warning'. I've never been able to put this second one into practice, as my life/career choices thus far have excluded looking after sheep or sailing. If I'm ever asked to take a herd of sheep across the English Channel though I'll have my eyes glued to the sky. I hope I'm not colour blind.

The Multiple Intelligence theory by Howard Gardner (*Frames of Mind*) is also a powerful way to help people understand their strengths, and much of this section is based on activities which explore his theory. Multiple Intelligences are used in Card Activities *Ace* to *9 of Hearts*. Here is a brief summary. Gardner first identified and introduced the idea of Multiple Intelligences around 25 years ago–a relief to all those with reservations about the limitations of IQ as a measure of intelligence and the disproportionate importance attached to maths and English in schools. They are often referred to as 'SMARTS' in education to simplify the terminology. I call them MINTs (Multiple INTelligences) just to be different. Giving someone the chance to be smart in eight broad ways instead of two has to be more positive and useful.

People MINT

Able to understand other people; their moods, desires, motivations. Getting along well with other people.

Self MINT

An understanding of yourself, your feelings, strengths and weaknesses. Confident, able to control your own emotions and stick to goals and targets.

Word MINT

An interest in words, reading, writing, discussion, jokes based on word play, telling and listening to stories.

Number MINT

Ability in maths and other logical thinking. Work sums out in their head, may enjoy brainteasers and puzzles. Like to ask/wonder why things are as they are.

Music MINT

Ability to understand and create music. Musicians, composers and dancers show a heightened musical intelligence, have good sense of rhythm. Like to listen to music whilst doing other activities.

Picture MINT

Ability to 'think in pictures' to see the visual world accurately, and recreate (or alter) it in the mind or on paper. Spatial intelligence is highly developed in artists, architects, designers and sculptors. Good with maps, graphs and charts or design and fashion, combining colours and styles.

Body MINT

Ability to use your body in a skilled way, for self-expression or toward a goal. Sports men and women, dancers and actors display this intelligence. Good co-ordination, can mimic others.

Nature MINT

Ability to understand the world of plants, minerals and animals. An enjoyment of the outdoors, animals, environment, conservation.

I also find that the work Robert Dilts has accomplished on Logical Levels is a fantastic framework for helping people think through their strengths, and I've included some activities based on this work in this section. There is a full description in Part Two.

Further activities in which you can explore MINTs include the following:

Ask people to think of jobs based around their strongest MINT and collate results. Challenge the group, in their teams, to suggest an occupation for each of the following: the best-paid; the most exciting; the most useful to society. They should all come up with worthy answers because *all* MINTs are valuable to society.

Many people say they are good at two or three MINTs, not just one. This is great and you can give people the opportunity to explore their own profile of MINTs and what this means for their choices of course/career.

You may also consider an activity for each MINT to help people appreciate the diversity of intelligence. Each card, 2 to 9, covers a separate MINT. Together they could support a half-day session. I have put groups into teams and then taken them through a series of challenges, teams competing against each other, to show the range of MINTs and have found that different group members will shine at different tasks.

Ace of Hearts: MINTed

This activity shows there are different ways to be successful. We don't have to be 'mint' at everything. Knowing our strengths can help us be our best.

This suit starts with an exploration of Multiple Intelligences (MINTs) which give people eight chances to be good at something instead of a narrow old-fashioned notion of intelligence based around IQ (mainly specific bits of maths and English) that labeled most people as thick (that is to say the 95% or so that didn't go to university during the last century).

A student told me of a careers lesson he attended recently in which the teacher asked the group 'What careers do you want to do?' One 13-year-old lad answered 'Professional footballer.' How would you reply? The teacher's response was, 'All footballers are stupid. Anyone got a better answer.' 'Teacher' may be his job title but I can't think of a more inappropriate word to describe what he is doing.

That teacher's definition of intelligence is too narrow and he is creating a hierarchy of intelligence. Both mistakes are costly. My favourite animal is the penguin. They appear clumsy and comical on land but in the water they are graceful and perfectly adapted to flourish. If we were simply to judge the penguin based on observing and testing it on land, perhaps a SAT for Antarctic seabirds, they would be perceived as thick and worthless. Everyone has talent and we can help them find it.

A

MINTed
Time: 10–15 mins

Activity: Place a description of each MINT around the room. (See page 63-4). Ask students to look at each then decide on their strongest and stand next to it. Allow four or five minutes. Ask each group to think of one person famous for using the MINT they are standing next to. For example, David Beckham — Body MINT, Madonna — Music MINT.

Learning Point: There are lots of ways to be clever, not just at maths and English, which schools tend to favour. You will be most successful if you find your strengths and use them in your work/life.

Preparation: See the introduction to the Hearts suit of cards for a description of Multiple Intelligences.

A

2 of Hearts: Number MINT

This is an activity designed to show that the many people who say they're rubbish at maths often do so because they simply don't know the tricks, techniques or rules that apply. Those gifted at maths understand these rules and can produce equations on a page that are as beautiful in their eyes as poetry is beautiful in the eyes of a words MINT person. You may want to read through this activity a few times just to make sure you are clear on each step. Please remember to ask for a volunteer tactfully. Ask, 'Is there anyone here who thinks they're bad at maths – because I want to prove to you that you're not.'

I asked this in one school and was initially greeted by silence. A teacher thought they'd help by pointing to a student and saying, 'John Green, you're useless at maths, why don't you volunteer?' His friends turned to him and laughed. Words are important. The group's experience of this activity will depend on the way you ask the question.

If you'd like to try something different, or feel you are on a roll and want to use another Number MINT activity, there is an example of a number illusion in the list of magic tricks starting on page 194.

Maths is so important, it is vital that we teach students to be competent in their confidence in the subject. Many people become almost phobic about it. Angela Clow, Professor of Psychophysiology at the University of Westminster, has developed experiments that measure the impact of thoughts on our bodies.

She measured infection-fighting antibodies after various activities and discovered that after smelling chocolate, listening to music or viewing art, levels increased, while after smelling rotten meat, or viewing distressing pictures, levels declined.

So, for many people maths is like rotten meat and can make them ill! We need ways to teach people that make them feel good whilst they're learning. The clue is in *Spades*.

2

Number MINT
Time: 5–10 mins

Activity:

1. Secretly ask one student who thinks they're not number smart for their year of birth (e.g. 1992).

2. Challenge the group to remember a sequence of four x five-digit numbers:

   19,921   99,219   92,199   21,992

3. Write the numbers on the board and cover them, reveal one at a time, then cover it.

4. Ask the group to remember the numbers, and they'll fail.

5. Now get your volunteer to write down the sequence of 20 digits and astound the group when you verify that it's correct. They've just written their year of birth five times.

Now get your volunteer to write down the whole sequence of 20 digits and astound the group when you verify it's correct. They've just written their year of birth five times.

Learning Point: We often think we're useless at something but it's because we don't know the 'tricks of the trade'. Many people then develop a blind spot and just stop trying. It happens to millions of people in maths but we do need to persevere with it, as it is important in all our lives.

Preparation: Volunteer needs to be found before activity starts or at the beginning.

2

3 of Hearts: Word MINT

Teaching this version of the NLP spelling strategy is a great way to start and finish a session.

The activity proves:

• We can all learn.

• We can all become better at spelling when we're shown how.

It's good to improve all our MINTs, not just discover those we're naturally best at.

When you ask people who consider themselves to be good spellers, 'What do you do in your head when you recall a word?', they tend to do the same thing. They picture the word, usually just above their eyeline, between 10 and 20 cm. They see the word written and they can even tell you the font and background. If it's a tough word they break it into chunks, check that the word feels right, and if it does, they know it's correct. If it doesn't feel right they go back and change a chunk in their head then check again until they are happy with it. This activity teaches 'poor spellers' the strategy that 'good spellers' use to spell well.

Make the activity as fun and as theatrical as possible. Encourage the group to applaud the volunteers up to the front, and again when they return to their seats. Do make sure the volunteers go through the steps for real, look them in the eye while you lead them to ensure you are burning this new learning into their brains. Only on one occasion has this activity not fully worked for me, and that was because I rushed through it too quickly. Otherwise it will work and it is a great 'convincer'.

'Convincers' are used in NLP to prove to people that what we are saying is true. You, as the teacher, are an expert. This helps when you then say to students they are talented and have potential; they are more likely to believe you! The convincer here can also be that they can learn and develop their brain and their potential. If you are not convinced, let me give you the medical analogy. We believe what doctors say because they are the experts. Stunts from *The Real Hustle* TV programme show that con artists often succeed after they have used 'convincers' such as a uniform or an official-looking letter.

1) You show correct spelling. Volunteer underlines 'para'.

2) Volunteer draws parachute + stick figure.

3) They write 'para' in different colour inside parachute.

4) They tear off their drawing.

5) They make it fly down 'through' the correct spelling of the word

6) LATER... they return and write up correct spelling!

Another activity which allows people to check out their word intelligence is to ask each team to find as many words as they can from the word 'INTELLIGENCE' in three minutes. I'd avoid spelling tests unless your group is comfortable with the idea and have not been traumatised in the past by being asked to spell words in front of the class. You'd be surprised how many people have suffered in this way and been put off returning to education as adults.

The activities within this suit, Jack, Queen and King, also use word MINT.

3

Word MINT
Time: 5 + 5 mins

Activity: Teach this version of the NLP Spelling Strategy.

Write up words SEPARATE and SEPERATE. This is one of the most commonly mis-spelt words. Ask for a vote on the correct version (usually around 50% for each one).

Ask for two volunteers who got it wrong to come out and show each volunteer that there's a 'para' in the middle, as in 'parachute' (point to it). They both draw a parachutist, using different coloured pens. They swap pens and write 'para' in the middle of the parachute they've drawn (this emphasises the letters and helps burn them into their visual memory, and does the same for those watching in the audience). They then tear their drawing from the flip chart and let the paper float down (with sound effects from you and the audience). This makes the experience fun, playful and memorable.

Ask them at the end of the session to spell the word and they will be able to!

Learning Point: We *can* learn, we *can* change our brain, we *can* improve — once we know how. Word MINT is a great activity to develop, as it plays a major part in our lives.

Preparation: None.

3

4 of Hearts: Picture MINT

Making an animal using foil or paper is a valuable activity because it reminds us of being at Primary school, which is when so many of us enjoyed our education. I apologise to anyone not allowed to make a foil or paper animal at Primary school and who may feel cheated and damaged. Perhaps you could sue, using of one those many firms of solicitors that advertise on daytime TV. Or you could do the activity now, using all the wisdom and experience you've gained in the intervening years.

I specify to groups that their creation must have at least four legs, to avoid the quick production of a snake or worm that takes less than five seconds to fashion. An additional or alternative way is to challenge them to draw animals – perhaps a pig, horse and sheep – with their 'wrong' hand. Most people can tell which is which, even when drawn with the wrong hand.

Many people label themselves as hopeless at drawing. Ask them where and when this belief began and they'll often say in a class-room. This is how many people learn they can't sing, spell or do maths. But we were not told how to be good in these areas. We need a strategy. The *Three of Hearts* explores 'I can't spell'. *Can't* is such a powerful word; the *Bonus Activity: Star Sign* will reveal why.

I saw NLP originator Richard Bandler stage an inspirational dem-onstration when he took someone who believed they couldn't draw, installed a strategy for drawing and then gave the man a paint brush, paper and paints and let him practise. The man produced some amazing work and was even offered £50 for his first painting, a brilliant landscape. He refused, not yet realising he could always paint another now that he knew how. He'd been told he couldn't draw by a teacher when he was 12 and he'd retained this belief until his mid-thirties. Bandler was kind about the teacher, saying perhaps she'd had an argument with her boyfriend that morning, or some-thing ...

4

Picture MINT
Time: 5-10 mins

Activity: Ask teams/groups to create a 3D animal with either tin foil or paper. It has to have four legs and be able to stand up, and you have to be able to guess what it is! Remind them to plan how they're going to approach the task.

Discussion after the task could include which other MINTs were needed for success.

And/or:

Ask the group to pair off and draw an animal with their 'wrong' hand; their partner then has to guess what it is. And/or ask for volunteers to come out to the front to try this.

'Picture smart' people tend to be good at this, even with their wrong hand.

(Hint: Picture smart people tend to imagine what they're drawing is already drawn on the paper and then trace over it.)

Learning Point: We all seem to enjoy this MINT, even if we're not brilliant at art. This is not usually the case with number and word MINT, where we're conditioned to feel bad about ourselves. (Although not when we're very young, when we learn how to speak by not being aware of our mistakes).

Preparation: Tin foil and/or paper.

4

5 of Hearts: Nature MINT

This is an intelligence best explored outdoors. If this is not possible then making a seed helicopter is an alternative activity. You may think this is straight from Primary school, but it is not. I know my daughter recently studied seed dispersal because she came home with a photocopied sheet of A4 with various questions about seed dispersal methods. I'm not knocking photocopied activities but they tend to rely on word intelligence, which is only one of many. There must be more interesting ways to explore seed dispersal than by using a photocopied A4 sheet.

Understanding our environment and how it works is rising up the hierarchy of importance as an intelligence. Up until around 200 years ago this would have probably been the most important MINT in Britain. In many countries across the world it still is. The impact of our lack of understanding about our environment and our place within it are brilliantly illustrated by explorers such as Bruce Parry and Ray Mears. David Attenborough, Bill Oddie and the late Steve Irwin also demonstrate the variety of ways we can appreciate our environment.

There is something about nature that soothes our soul. When people write a list of things that make them happy (*Nine of Hearts*) being outdoors often features. It's inspiring to gaze at mountains, the sky, the sea, take a walk in a forest, or lie on a beach feeling the warmth of the sun on our bodies. It connects us to our world and our place within it. I'll let Charles Darwin continue, he was blessed in nature MINT:

'In my journal I wrote that whilst standing in the grandeur of a Brazilian forest, it's not possible to give an adequate idea of the higher feelings of wonder, admiration and devotion, which fill and elevate the mind. There is more in man than the mere breath of his body. A state of mind connected to a sense of sublimity.'

From *Darwin's Worms** by Adam Phillips

* Some books are better than their titles, Darwin studied worms you see. It does not refer to a medical condition

5

Nature MINT
Time: 5–10 mins

Activity: Make a seed helicopter.

Cut out a capital T shape then fold as shown below.

Fly the helicopter.

Discuss how you could improve the design, how you would distribute seeds if you were a plant, go out and find seeds, or bring in some other examples, discuss movement in different species.

Learning Point: People with this MINT don't get to use it or develop it much at school.

Luckily, there are many courses/careers that require nature MINT.

Preparation: Paper, scissors.

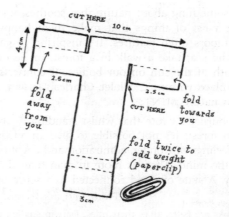

6 of Hearts: Body MINT

This intelligence is probably the most underrated in academic circles, perhaps because body MINT is experienced in our stomachs and bodies. It's fascinating to listen to body MINT people describe what happens when they're at their best. They *feel* rhythm, movement and let go of conscious control of their bodies and allow it to move in synchronicity and synergy with their surroundings – like electricity, according to *Billy Elliot*, the film about the boy star ballet dancer.

Academic MINT (maths and English) is experienced in and around our heads. It is conscious and separate from the body. This is why academic people are often embarrassing on the dance floor, writhing uncomfortably and out of synch with the music. My driving instructor once said to me that he noticed that 'brainy' people usually take longer to learn to drive than 'normal' people. This was just after I'd failed my driving test for the third time and I like to think he was giving me a compliment.

I'm also hopeless at making, constructing and building things. Activities such as putting up a tent or assembling a bed bring me out in a sweat and make my family very wary of sampling my handy work. My son slept uneasily at the top of the bunk bed I'd made for him, nervously expecting it to collapse during the night.

We should attempt to improve our skill levels in all MINTs. We never know when we might need them. It's not good enough to say 'Oh, I've never been good at Maths, sport or ironing.' I tried the last one, but my wife was having none of it. I took up karate with my children to help me develop my body intelligence. My progress was far slower than the 7-year-olds girls I trained with, but I did get better over time. I gave up in the end as I was beaten too easily by the girls during the sparring at the end of each session. I could handle the humiliation but it was too embarrassing for my children to watch. I only realised this when my 8-year-old daughter offered to 'sort' one of the other girls for me.

Academic people should remember how excruciatingly painful it can be to perform physical challenges, as this is how many body MINT people feel in school, trapped behind desks unable to move. Some academics may sneer at body MINT people but society rewards many richly; not just the sports stars.

The physical challenge presented here is fairly tame but illustrates the point.

The hierarchy of intelligences usually starts with 'number' and 'word' at the top and 'body' at the bottom, and metal work seems to be bottom of the body smart subjects. Research by Ken Robinson suggests this is repeated in all educational systems across the world and not just in the UK. When the Bronze Age started, metal work must have been the most exciting and useful subject to study (though not much use *before* the Bronze Age!). Ranking subjects only results in ranking people, and it isn't the best answer.

At school, did you ever have to stand against a cold wall waiting to be picked by two team captains?

We quickly discover our place in the pecking order of body MINT using this method.

Some people are scarred by this process. If you are picked last you could feel bad for years. The same kind of experience occurs every day for many 'non-academic' children at school each time they go into the 'bottom' class in maths, English or whatever.

The right wing press bemoan the trendy no-failure culture of schools. In my experience this is a myth. Most children are too quick to label themselves as 'thick' or 'stupid'. I'm yet to meet a teenager able to list more things that they are good at than things they are bad at.

How confident are you as a teacher and role model?

In Paul McKenna's *I Can Make You Rich*, he describes this scenario.

Imagine you have applied for a job that you really want and believe you could do really well in all of the tasks involved.

Imagine the salary you'd expect. Your first interview was great; the panel liked your ideas and said so. At your second interview they offer you the job but the salary is more than you thought. The actual salary has an extra zero on the end. For example, instead of £40,000 it's £400,000.

What is your reaction?

Some people don't feel they could take the job.

Your response reveals much about your attitude towards money, your own self-worth and your belief in your skills.

6

Body MINT
Time: 5–10 mins

Activity: Low wire act.

Challenge students to walk convincingly along a drawn or imaginary rope, line or wire, as if they are going to fall and with maximum drama. All must have a go and all vote for the best. Body smart people are usually good at balancing and controlling their bodies. An alternative is to challenge them to throw scrunched up paper into a bin. Again, body MINT people tend to be better at this challenge. Obviously, this task has inherent risk!

Learning Point: This MINT is generally not used/developed/ valued in much of the school curriculum. People with this MINT often learn best by being active and can be frustrated sitting still in lessons.

Do the students agree? Are some MINTs better than others?

Preparation: Rope/Paper (optional).

6

7 of Hearts: Music MINT

Playing a pop quiz, or asking students to identify the theme to certain TV programmes or advertisements, gives music MINTs a chance to shine. Older people (ah-hem, let's say 40-plus) love the little trip down memory lane afforded by this game; you can almost hear the crunch of Werthers Originals as they rummage through the dusty recesses of their minds. Another version is to play music and ask what moods each piece evokes. The theme from *Rocky* or *Star Wars* evokes a ready-for-battle mood, whereas the theme for comedy programmes is usually jolly, quirky and clumsy. Larry David said he searched for ages to identify an appropriate piece of music for the theme to *Curb your Enthusiasm* and heard an advert when traveling abroad that was perfect. He tracked down the music and it perfectly captures the mood of the programme. Music goes straight into our core in a way other communication does not.

You can witness the powerful effect of music at a wedding reception disco. Notice the stampede of middle-aged women to the dance floor once they hear the first few bars of *Gypsies, Tramps and Thieves* by Cher, or *I Am What I Am* by Gloria Gaynor. Normally polite and restrained women begin dancing with the enthusiasm and gay abandon normally associated with hallucinogenic substances.

When I explore MINTs with teachers (*Ace of Hearts*) many more are word and people MINT than the other MINTs. This is not the result with teenagers. Many more teenagers are body and music MINT (up to half in most groups) yet these two are least used in schools. As Homer Simpson would say: 'Doh!'

Advantages of using music include:

• Embeds learning faster and deeper.
• Brings groups together (rapport, bonding, energising).
• Stimulates and focuses creativity.
• Calms down 'hyper' students.

For more on using music see Eric Jensen's *Superteaching* or *The Little Book of Music for the Classroom* by Independent Thinking Associate, Nina Jackson.

7

Music MINT
Time: 5–10 mins

Activity: Play 'Name That Tune' using the first bars (some iPods have a version of this built into the extras section). Music MINTs are usually very good at this.

You'll need to bring in some music; you may need to buy some if your recent purchases tend to be compilation albums that remind you of your time at college!

Or you can ask students to say what emotions they feel when listening to pieces of music such as the *Star Wars* soundtrack or the *Benny Hill* theme.

Learning Point: Music MINTs tend to be good at recognising tunes, instruments etc.

They can often hold a tune better than many *X Factor* contestants. They may learn best by developing song lyrics that convey important subject information.

We all appreciate music and are affected by it, whether we like the music or not.

Preparation.

Music CD for Pop Quiz.

Theme tunes CD/download for mood activity.

7

8 of Hearts: People MINT

We can all benefit from developing this intelligence. It has been well researched and described using many different labels, such as Emotional Intelligence or EQ , interpersonal skills, women's intuition, bedside manner, red thinking hat, and many others. The concept took a bit of a bashing during the 1980s when Thatcherism's individualistic mantra coldly gripped much of the UK. It is interesting that many societies stress the importance of this intelligence and its development far more than so-called developed countries.

A lack of this intelligence can inhibit our performance, even if we're brilliant in some of the others. Dr Andrew Curran, Independent Thinking associate and author of *The Little Book of Big Stuff About the Brain*, has produced statistics that suggest doctors, teachers and managing directors can display a high lack of EQ that does a great disservice to those people they represent, as well as to themselves.

Watching the difficulty many on the autistic spectrum have in understanding sarcasm, jokes, empathy, body language, facial expressions and feelings illustrates the importance of this intelligence.

The mood reading activity is a great introduction to this intelligence. The aim is to ask students to identify different moods. There is an interesting idea, known as 'primary emotions theory', that suggests all emotions originate from a mix of the following six: anger, disgust, fear, sadness, joy and surprise.

The Body Language Book, by Barbara and Allan Pease, provides further examples of reading body language that can help students explore and improve their people MINT. The chapter on smiling is particularly interesting and accessible to teenagers. Can you spot the difference between a real smile and a fake smile? Most people can.

I occasionally ask a group which MINT is the most useful. This one is usually the joint winner. If you're not sure how to develop this MINT the following advice from Aldous Huxley could help. He was speaking at a conference towards the end of his life. The delegates were anticipating a lengthy address. He simply said,

'I'm very embarrassed because I've worked for forty years, I've studied everything around, I did experiments, went to several countries and all I can tell you is to be just a little kinder to each other.'

8 People MINT
Time: 10–15 mins

Activity: There's a number of versions of this, depending on your own confidence and that of your group. The simple version (i.e. least work required in the classroom by you or your students) is to prepare a DVD with short clips of people expressing different moods and ask the group to identify each, including some easy ones such as happy, sad, anger, love, relaxed, and the more subtle, envy, jealousy, regret.

Alternatively, a short clip from *EastEnders* or a scene from a Shakespeare DVD will probably suffice.

Another version is to write down a series of moods on slips of paper. Arrange students in groups of around six in a circle and secretly ask one student to peek at their piece of paper, get into the mood, then give a present (a scrunched up piece of paper will do) to someone in the group, saying 'John,' (or their name if it isn't John), 'I'd really like to give you this present now and it took me ages to choose it for you'. The rest of the group then has to guess the mood. Angry, excited and bored are easy to guess but some of the others are not so easy.

Learning Point: We can all do with developing this MINT.

It is crucial to our success in life generally.

Are females naturally better at this than males?

Preparation: Video Clips from *EastEnders* or Shakespeare.

Moods written on sheets of paper, or you can ask the students to do this.

8

9 of Hearts: Self MINT

The 'happy list' activity is inspired by the research conducted by Greg Hicks and Rick Foster in *How We Choose to Be Happy*. They identified nine things happy people have in common. One of them is knowing what makes them happy and taking a conscious decision to undertake these activities. They should be acts that don't harm yourself or anyone else (these tend to provide short-term pleasure but long-term pain). As a follow on, I often suggest that students ask friends and family to draw up their own lists and compare them. What activities do they have in common?

You can also ask them to identify which activities they can do more of in the next few weeks to show how their happiness can be increased. People are generally surprised at how many of the things on their list are quite simple: walking the dog, a night out with friends, and watching a good film are common answers. If you ask teenage lads, don't be surprised at a few honest answers. Personally, I'm quite impressed they can spell 'masturbation' as they usually say they're not word MINT ...

Foster and Hicks' book has a great ending covering the concept of synergy. The word describes the idea that the whole is greater than the sum of its parts. Do all the stuff covered in this book and you may experience synergy, when $1 + 1 = 3$, perhaps. My favourite example of synergy is about nurses working with poor people in South Africa with HIV/Aids. They were being treated with a local plant, because they couldn't afford the preferred drugs. The plant worked as well as the drugs but the scientists couldn't understand why, because the active ingredient was inert in the plant. They realised the plant had a kind of washing-up liquid in it, in addition to the active ingredient, which meant that when the plant was prepared it released the active element and made it work. These two features of the plant worked together to produce effective and unexpected results.

In the 2005 TV programme *Making Slough Happy*, rather than asking participants to identify their own sources of happiness, they were given a Top Ten list. Many are embedded within activities in this book but here are few of the others that you could try:

- Physical exercise.
- Smile at and/or say hello to a stranger.
- Cut down the amount of TV you watch by 50%.
- Plant something and keep it alive.

The last one reminds me of an answer the comedian Ken Dodd gave when asked by Michael Parkinson, 'What's the secret of happiness?'

His reply was: 'Grow something, grow a business, your family, something important to you.'

In a talk on www.ted.com, Dan Gilbert poses the following question:

Who is happier one year after the event:

(a) A lottery Winner (a large win)

(b) Someone involved in an accident in which they permanently lose the use of their legs?

For the answer turn over the page.

The answer is both are equally happy.

I train staff in organisations that advise adults made to reconsider career/life following major accidents; they confirm Gilbert's quoted research.

9

Self MINT
Time: 5-10 mins

Activity: Write a list of all the things you do that make you happy (that don't harm anyone, including yourself). Tick any you could do more of and you'll increase your happiness. Which other people are involved? Look after them, as they're important to your happiness.

Learning Point: Happy people know what activities make them happy and they actively plan to do those things. It is better to focus in a positive direction rather than think about all the things we don't like.

Preparation: A sheet of A4 for each student.

9

10 of Hearts: Identity

The next cards cover logical levels, as described in Part Two.

Using identity words as a starting point, ask groups to agree on three words that apply to all of the group (e.g. learner, child, British) and three words that apply only to themselves as individuals (e.g. explorer, leader, drummer) and no one else within their group.

Explain that research suggests successful people tend to have a clear idea of their identity. This means they know who they are and the things that are important in their lives. They are then able to live their lives positively within a secure sense of who they are and where they are going. Our sense of identity is like a compass, which can reassure us that we're going along on the right lines, or alert us to the times we may not be being true to ourselves. We can change plans and tactics (by developing our skills and behaviour or changing our environment) throughout our life to ensure we do not compromise our identity.

Stephen Covey presents an interesting version of this in *7 Habits of Highly Effective People*. He stresses the need for us to have a sense of our own identity, otherwise we risk living our lives to make others happy. An example of potential compromises that can impede a healthy sense of identity is being part of a family, gang or religion. Membership of these groups could result in pressure being applied to influence us to harm ourselves or others.

10

Identity
Time: 5–10 mins

Activity: Challenge each individual to think of something only they will believe to be true out of the whole the group and to think of something the whole group will believe to be true.

You can check after three to five minutes if anyone was successful.

It's quite hard!

And/or:

Ask individuals to identify which identity words they are attracted to. (See Logical Levels in Part Two).

And/or:

What tribes/groups do you belong to? What beliefs does the group share?

(British, European, religious, gang, youth club, family, football team, school, Tufty Club ...)

Learning Point: Our beliefs about who we are and our sense of identity are like an internal compass that we can use to help us make informed decisions.

The groups we link ourselves to have an impact on our beliefs and identity.

Preparation: Awareness of Identity words in Part Two.

10

Jack of Hearts: Personality Words

This activity can link in with the *Speed Dating* activity. As an additional activity, or as a replacement, you can choose from the list of behaviour words instead of personality words listed in Part Two.

Ask students to describe the qualities they most admire in others. Ask who their role models are and why. Build a picture of people at their best. Ask people to relate this to themselves. What challenges have they faced in the past and how have they overcome them? These kinds of questions can only be explored with some groups but the results can be very positive for everyone. I'm amazed at the strength, compassion, wisdom and generosity many young people can share – teenagers overcoming personal and family tragedy and much more.

A headteacher once told me she was about to tear into a Year 10 student who was frequently sent to her for not having a pen. Just before she started on her well-rehearsed rant on school ethos and the importance of rules, the girl, who usually just took a telling off on the chin, said, 'Look, I'm looking after my alcoholic mum, I have to get my little sister dressed and to school before I come here. I was cleaning up sick this morning and you're going to slag me off for not having a pen!' The headteacher gave her one of her own pens instead of a reprimand. If we can help people recognise their own strengths we're really helping them glimpse their true potential. As a visitor to schools, I rarely delve as deep as this, but if you do establish relationships with people over time you are able to help them in amazing ways.

When I'm with a group I usually tell stories of people who have done amazing things instead of asking for their own stories. Our behaviour is the way we express our identity, personality and values and it is something we can all control. The qualities we admire most in others are often the ones we would most like to develop within ourselves.

Hearts – Know Your Strengths

J

Personality Words
Time: 5-10 mins

Activity: Ask people to choose the three words that most accurately match how they see themselves and three words they'd like to become a bigger part of who they are over the next few years. If you trust the group, ask them to suggest words (from the list, as this has only positive words to choose from — see Logical Levels in Part Two) that they think reflect the personality strengths of their peers.

Learning Point: We're all interested in ourselves and even more interested in what others think of us. Have peers chosen the same words as we've chosen for ourselves? Ask each other why they chose the words they did. It is useful to assess our own strengths and qualities and to find out what others think are our natural strengths.

Preparation: Personality words in Part Two.

J

Queen of Hearts: Strength Test

This activity sums up the section very well. We need to seek feedback about our strengths, beliefs, plans and dreams. This is the way to build an accurate picture of who we are. By exploring our beliefs at all of the Logical Levels (see Part Two), not just our current skills, we can make really informed choices. Successful people seem to be almost compulsive about receiving feedback and using it to grow as a person.

Virgin boss Richard Branson is quoted as saying he has never failed in his life. When reminded of his company's unsuccessful bid to run the National Lottery, he said that it couldn't be considered a failure because the things he learned putting together the bid earned him contracts worth millions of pounds over the next few years. Believing in yourself, then discovering and developing your strengths, is a powerful combination. Another multi-millionaire, the publisher Felix Dennis, gives similar advice for anyone interested in a career in publishing: go and work for a publisher and find out as much as you can about the business. Later, you can then run your own business applying what you've learned. The same principle applies to whatever career appeals to you.

Many successful people suggest luck plays a part in their success. When you delve a little deeper it appears luck has very little to do with it. Seeking and using feedback is a recurring theme amongst achievers, for personal and business success. In the book *How They Started*, by David Lester, the author interviews people who have created enviable business empires. This activity explores what they have in common.

Karan Bilimoria, founder of Cobra Beer, puts it in a nutshell: 'Never, ever go forward with an idea without actually testing it out on the consumer first.' His advice to entrepreneurs is to build a brand and then you can think of yourself as a unique brand that you need to understand before you unleash it on the world.

Q

Strength Test
Time: 5-10 mins

Activity: Ask students to identify things they can do to help enhance their self-awareness in the next week/month. It could be any of the following:

- Ask three people who know you what they think you should do with your life?
- Try something new (a skill, activity, visit a new place ...).
- Do something for someone else (random acts of kindness make us feel better).

They should write down their objectives. Research suggests this is a habit of successful people.

Hold the group to one of these challenges and share feedback.

Learning Point: It is only by trying new ideas that we discover new stuff about ourselves. We can live like a weed growing weakly between a crack in the wall unable to move, or we can explore and experience the world around us and grow. Once we expand our awareness we can have a plan.

Preparation: None.

Q

King of Hearts: Dry River Crossing

I not only use all the brains I have but all I can borrow.

Woodrow Wilson

This is an indoor version of the 'build a life raft and sail across a river as a team' exercise or the 'build a tower out of a box of materials'. You need a hall and equipment, such as trays, pieces of wood, coats, newspapers.

Each team has to cross the hall without anybody touching the floor. To win, they must decide how they will work together. This kind of activity is great fun, active and memorable. It requires teamwork and skill using a wide range of MINTs. It replicates the world of work fairly well, as it is task-focused and success depends on the participants themselves rather than a handbook.

Make sure each team has an equal amount of material and that dangerous items are not included.

K

Dry River Crossing
Time: 30 mins

Activity: Teams of students have to race across the hall (or outside across a field). They each have a selection of equipment to use. They must all cross the designated area without anyone touching the floor. They must decide how to work together and how to cross, all at once or in sections.

Make sure the items only cover around a quarter of the distance (see Preparation). This activity is best with large teams.

It tends to work best if you select teams randomly.

Learning Point: To be successful, this activity requires qualities such as teamwork, skill, quick thinking, leadership, and creativity.

What did you learn about yourself during the activity?

Preparation: You'll need a box of flat, safe items for each team that cover roughly a quarter of the distance they are expected to navigate.

K

CLUBS

Have a Plan

Have a Plan

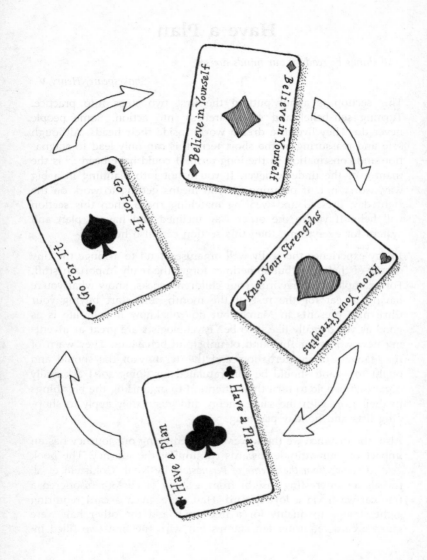

Believe in Yourself

Go For It

Know Your Strengths

Have a Plan

Have a Plan

All things be ready if our minds are so.

Shakespeare, Henry V

This section is about putting the first two steps into practice. Turning self-belief and self-awareness into action. Some people never do. They live in a dream world inside their heads. Although safe and reassuring in the short term this can only lead to stagnation and constipation in the long term. 'I could have been ...' is the mantra of the underachiever. If you're not into planning in a big way, worry not. If planning for you means getting to work on the right day, dressed and wearing matching shoes, then this section will help. If you're the other way inclined and have a plan and system for everything, then this section can also help.

In my experience the really well organised tend to arrange the tiny details of their lives but sometimes forget the really important stuff. For example, you may iron your children's socks, know what you're having to eat for the rest of the month, and start buying your Christmas presents in March, but do you know if your life is as good as you'd really like it to be? Psychologists are great at inventing new words for this kind of unhelpful behaviour. They warn of the 'dangers of musterbation' and the 'tyranny of the should and ought to' – and should be congratulated for doing so. I ask really organised people to turn their attention to organising the big things in their lives with the same energy and gusto they apply to shopping lists and holiday planning.

Also, the distance we think we've traveled along our journey has an impact on our attitude towards continuing the journey. The book *Yes! 50 Secrets from the Science of Persuasion*, by Noah Goldstein et al, reveals an interesting insight from a study of customers offered a free car-wash via a loyalty card. Half were given a card requiring eight stamps to qualify for a free wash and the other half were given a card requiring ten stamps but with the first two filled in.

Did this make a difference, even though both groups required the same number of stamps to qualify for the free wash?

Yes it did, in two ways. The group given the first two of 10 returned in far greater numbers *and* more quickly than those given a blank card. How can we use this to motivate students? Emphasise the distance a student has already traveled and the effort already invested: 'You've been doing this subject for three years and have just two to go.' 'You've produced great work up until now and you need to submit just two more assignments.'

Writing ten years ago, in *All Our Futures*, John Abbott said, 'Life is more than work. If we give children the idea that they need high level skills only for work, we have got it all wrong. They are going to need even higher level skills to perform in a democratic society. We have got to get this absolutely right: the issue is not technology but what it means to be human, what kind of future we want for the human race.' Similarly, university is not just a good idea because your earning potential is likely to increase if you're a graduate. It's a good idea to explore the positive impact of going to university in other areas of our lives and not just financial reward. (Indeed, recent research suggests the earning premium of a degree could be far lower than the figure of £240,000 total per person often quoted.)

I've learned that everyone wants to live on top of the mountain, but all the happiness and growth occurs while you're climbing it.

Andy Rooney, American journalist

Sometimes following a plan makes us realise it was not in fact a good plan. This is still a good result, as we have discovered useful information for the bigger journey. Most of us plod along at way below our full potential. It's as if we're saying to ourselves, 'Well, I could have a great life but I just can't be arsed at the moment,' and we look for reasons to justify our sloth: '*EastEnders* is on soon, I'll wait until the kids are older, I'm too old, I'm too young ...' In my experience more people under aspire rather than over aspire.

If we continually try to force a child to do what he's afraid to do, he will become more timid, and will use his brains and energy not to explore the unknown, but to find ways to avoid the pressures we put on him.

John Holt, How Children Learn

So the key is to start planning after acquiring belief in ourselves and an accurate knowledge of our strengths. If we plan when we're feeling timid then our plans will be timid. If we plan when we're feeling good about ourselves our plans might just be as bold and bright as our real potential.

This cuts to the heart of the debate about the purpose of school and education. On *Question Time* recently the panel was asked: Should parents be thrown into prison if their children truant? Monty Don and Kelvin McKenzie admirably articulated the polarised views of Middle Britain. In which camp do you sit?

Monty Don	**Kelvin McKenzie**
School as apprenticeship	School as factory/military
Educate children for life	Train children for jobs
Child as Learners (creative, reflective, team-workers, independent thinkers)	Child as pupil (punctual, compliant, competitive)
Child nurtured to achieve their full potential	Child as winner or loser in jobs/life

Perhaps you are in neither camp. If you'd rather make your own camp I admire your independent thinking skills and ability to challenge potentially false choices put to you. Of course this does mean you've been in Monty's camp with me and the other hippies.

Schools and teachers are asked to serve the wishes of parents and politicians sitting in both camps. That's before anyone asks the children what they want.

Ace of Clubs: Percentages

It is said that we only use 20% of our full potential. Ask students, 'How much are you using?'

Ask them to identify how much potential they have tapped into so far, on a line from zero through to 100%. Say it's OK wherever they find themselves now. The important thing is to be honest with themselves. It's where they go from here that's important. Tell each student to think of what they would have to do to increase by 10%. Ask them to imagine doing it, then physically moving along the line.

What about being at 100%? There is a vogue in sport, especially football, for managers and players to say they or their team are giving 110% or 150%; I think I even heard Kevin Keegan say one of his lads never gives less than 1000%. I use 100% as the maximum, but like the Spinal Tap amp that went up to 11 rather than 10, you may need to be flexible. If someone says to me they give 120% in their chosen sport I ask what percentage they give in other parts of their lives – and the point is made.

This activity reminds us we need to know where we're at now before working out where we want to go. This question presupposes most people are not achieving their full potential. Most will estimate between 20% and 60%. Ask someone what would happen if they used 10% more and what effect that would have on their life? What if they went all the way to 100%? They're being invited to look into a more positive future. If they don't know, they need to go back to the previous step and develop greater self-awareness, though even a rough plan is better than no plan. A ship sailing somewhere specific is less likely to drift or get lost than a ship without a destination.

This activity links well with the *8 of Diamonds: First Date*.

A

Percentages
Time: 5-10 mins

Activity: According to a survey, people use on average about 20% of their potential. Ask students how much they are using.

Ask them to identify how much of their potential they are currently tapping into, on a line from zero to 100%. Say it's OK where you are now, it's good to be honest with yourself, because it's where you go from here that's important.

Ask each student to think of what they'd have to do to increase by 10%? Ask them to imagine doing this and what it feels like. Is it do-able? Does it feel good? What about being at 100%? What would they achieve/do if they were there?

Learning Point: We generally stay within our comfort zone.

It's useful to think about moving out of it. We can do this by thinking about what will happen if we do, what resources we have (within us, friends, family, mentors), what extra resources or training or experience we need to be tapping into more of our potential.

Preparation: None.

 A

2 of Clubs: Wheels on Fire

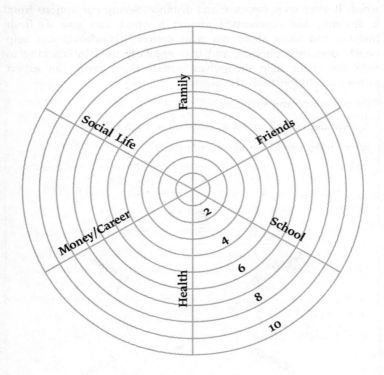

An idea popular in coaching is to ask people to rate different areas of their lives. This helps to focus on what is important to them now and in the future. For example a teenager may decide to go to college for social reasons (to make more friends, have fun, join clubs, play sport ...) but can see on their 'wheel' that college will also help in other areas, such as family and career prospects.

Clubs – Have a Plan

The first step is to assess where we are now and the next is to take a look at the result. In NLP terms this 'dissociates' us, in other words it gives us perspective and distance. Seeing our options from a distance, and represented around a wheel, can give us fresh insights and ideas about our next option. Dissociation can help people overcome phobias, and it is regularly used in coaching to help the client help themselves, rather than having an expert impose a solution from the outside.

Do we notice any surprises?

Are we doing well in some areas more than others?

What areas would we like to improve?

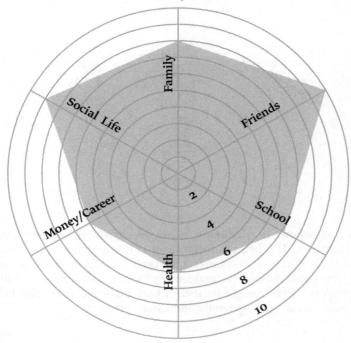

The third step is to think of things we can do to improve the areas we'd like to improve. Look at the impact of each action on all of the wheel. If someone decides they'd like to improve their career by working longer hours, will the impact on family life be acceptable? The wheel allows us to take a snapshot of our life, assess where we'd like to make changes and explore the implications of each potential change.

The categories for the wheel – career, family, friends, health, money, home – can be changed to suit different groups.

2

Wheels on Fire
Time: 10 mins

Activity: Provide each student with a Wheel of Life.

Ask them to choose six areas of their lives they would like to explore. Each is written along a spoke of the wheel. They then assess each area out of 10 (10 being brilliant, through to 0, absolutely pants) and mark it on their wheel. When they join the points they will have a representation of how well they're doing in their lives.

To follow on ask questions such as:

- Are there any surprises?
- Which bits would you like to work on?
- What can you do to improve those areas?

Learning Point: We can assess all the different parts of our lives and consider the impact they have on each other. One person could be doing really well in their job but not seeing much of their family. The snapshot can be changed. After all, we can influence our lives more than anyone else!

Preparation: Wheel of Life for everyone.

2

3 of Clubs: Pictures of You

This activity is best done over a half an hour or so, if delivered as described. If you'd like a quicker version, short cuts are highlighted. Another way to unleash dreams and ambitions in a creative process is to ask your group to look through magazines and newspapers to produce a montage of how they would like to be in five or ten years time. This tends to provide more interesting results than something such as a skills audit. I've tried both. There are many different versions of this activity.

I saw a group of Year 10 students being asked to draw a typical university student, as part of a raising aspiration day, which brought out all the stereotypes quickly and safely. I like versions that make this task personal. You don't have to use magazines; just drawing and labeling yourself can work effectively but the act of tearing (or cutting, if you can trust your group with scissors) and gluing seems more satisfying – perhaps as it transports us back to those light, sunny care-free primary schooldays before the burden of teenage angst began to weigh heavily on our slumped shoulders. Peeling dried glue from our hands seems to be a universally satisfying experience that combines all the fun and excitement of picking a scab without the potential pain of a picked-too-soon wound and the 'you should have left it alone' voice of your mum in your head.

This activity dissociates us from the act of assessing ourselves. It is a technique often used in NLP, and many forms of therapy and conflict resolution, because we see ourselves for real with this additional distance and perspective. Another classic version of this technique is getting people to write their own obituaries and asking how they'd like to be remembered. I was nearly in tears once when a hard lad, keen to join the Army, said he wanted to be remembered for making his mum proud of him.

3

Pictures of You
Time: 15–30 mins

Activity: Each student produces a montage depicting how they will be in five years time if everything goes really well. If they struggle, remind them of the life categories from the previous activity, *2 of Clubs*.

Learning Point: One of the habits of successful people is they think about the best that could happen, not the worst. They then identify steps to make it happen. Which bits of your montage are most important to you? Why? What would make you most proud?

Preparation: You'll need plenty of glossy magazines, glue and scissors.

Ask permission to raid the neighbour's recycling to save yourself some money.

3

4 of Clubs: Time After Time

Time may be infinite but the amount of time we have on this planet certainly isn't. A plan can ensure we make the most of it. This activity turns our attention to the big stuff, the big picture. Students match the activity to the average time in years spent doing each activity.

An interesting discussion can follow this simple activity. The main learning point is that people do not spend much time planning their lives. This activity links well with *4 of Diamonds: Paper Wait*.

There was an interesting story in the press about a window cleaner who thought he was an inventor. If he were asked what his job was, he'd say 'inventor' and his mates would laugh and say, 'No he isn't an inventor, he's a window cleaner'. On holiday in Florida he saw a TV news item about a little girl who died from an allergic reaction to a wasp sting. She'd drunk from a can of fizzy drink and hadn't realised a wasp had got inside the can. As she took a drink it went inside her mouth and stung her. Tragically, a number of children in the USA die each year this way. The window cleaner was upset and returned home thinking there must be something that could be done to prevent this sort of accident. He pottered around in his shed a while and came up with a sort of mesh that covers the drinking hole. This would allow liquid to flow but prevent insects entering the can. Can manufacturers like the idea and he'll probably earn loads of money when cans are manufactured using his invention. This man had self-belief, a knowledge of his strengths and once he found a suitable challenge he could plan and go for it. This is the process we can all use to ensure we achieve our best.

4

Time After Time
Time: 5–8 mins

Activity: Students are asked to match an activity to the time spent on it during an average lifetime.

Guess which five activities take up the following time spans during the average lifetime:

30 years

15 years

4 years

3 years

2 hours

These are whole years when all the time on the activity is added together.

Answers: 30 sleeping, 15 working, 4 eating, 3 at school, 2 planning our lives/future.

Learning Point: Without being morbid — we have limited lifetime!

We spend very little time planning the very important stuff.

Preparation: None.

4

5 of Clubs: Money, Money, Money

A good plan is based on sound information. We need to research our plans. For many people a strong motivator is money. This activity challenges our knowledge of salaries for five fairly well-known jobs. I sometimes ask, 'What's the best thing that could happen to you?' and the usual answer is, 'Win the lottery'. This is an understandable response because it appears to require the least effort for the greatest gain. I suspect a detailed cost/benefit analysis, taking into account how many tickets you'd need to purchase (time and money) for potential winnings compared to the time and cost of studying for a Law degree (or other worthy goals), would perhaps favour the latter.

I sometimes remind people that if they earned £25,000 a year, during their full working life they'd earn £1 million. Unfortunately we don't *feel* like a millionaire due to the spread-out nature of the way we earn our salaries. I suppose you could try asking to be paid up front for the full 40 years.

We generally don't spend enough time collecting enough information to make well-informed decisions. I've stayed in some holiday accommodation that has been unsuitable. This probably could have been avoided with a little more research. A teenage girl recently revealed to me her plan was to marry a premiership footballer and be a 'WAG' living in London. Her number one choice is Thierry Henry. At the time of our conversation he wasn't playing in London so a little further research would have revealed the flaw in her plan.

During this activity you may be asked to reveal your own salary. I deal with this by replying, 'Great question! The purpose of this game is to encourage research, so if you're interested go and find out'.

Clubs – Have a Plan

5
Money, Money, Money
Time: 5-10 mins

Activity: Match the monthly salary to the job.

These are correct amounts, so mix them up or the session will be slower and less exciting and quick.

- Doctor £5000
- Paramedic £2500
- Plumber £2000
- UK average £2000
- Taxi driver £1000
- Hairdresser £750

NB: Teacher is the same as paramedic but without the sense of excitement. You may want to share that with them or you may want to keep it to yourself.

These figures (excluding overtime, tips and bonuses) are from the *2006 Annual Survey, Office for National Statistics*.

Learning Point: Money is important. Many people make career choices without checking out salaries, prospects, hours of work, how much they'll need for the lifestyle they desire etc.

Research is an important part of planning — it leads to informed decisions.

Preparation: None.

5

6 of Clubs: Walk This Way

This activity requires enough space to allow a few people to walk in a straight line for around 20 steps but, like a Jamie Oliver recipe, this activity can be adapted. The purpose is to illustrate the simple point that it's useful to know where you're going – then you'll avoid obstacles and arrive sooner. The alternative is a random approach and bruised shins.

Children do need to be shown the way. When they're young, they believe adults know the answers to everything. Even when we're old enough to know better we still seek out advice, hoping someone will know the answer. Offering advice to help people find their own answers is the tricky way, but really is the only way. The right pace helps. I was laughing out loud while reading Stuart Maconie's excellent book *Pies and Prejudice*, and my daughter asked what I was laughing at. I recounted the bit where Stuart – I'm calling him Stuart but I don't really know him, I hope that's OK – says when he enters a museum he starts at a slow pace, giving each glass cabinet and plaque* his full attention and respect, but his pace quickens as his interest diminishes and by the time he reaches the gift shop he's practically jogging. I'm laughing again at the picture of his guilty little face as he runs through the gift shop for the exit.

My daughter said it's the other way round for her. And so it is. She enters a museum, quickly scans round to see if there's any clothes

---

* I've never understood why toothpaste manufacturers have been allowed to use the word plaque to describe something horrible when its other use is generally associated with dignity and tribute to fallen heroes etc. Similarly, Chlamydia sounds lovely, like something pensioners should admire hanging gracefully from trellis in their back garden. Does plaque really exist? We believe experts. Ah, the power of a white lab coat and a diagram showing something bad stopped by something good. We believe so many things without understanding them. These things are important when we decide which path to walk.

to try on (the more museums resemble Next or New Look the better their attendances will be with the teenage girl demographic) then makes a dash for the gift shop. Her Mum and I, on the other hand, not wanting to show disrespect to the odd-looking security man sat on an uncomfortable chair in the corner, wonder what is the minimum amount of time we can spend before we head off for the café. My wife usually starts a conversation with the guard to compensate for our children's thinly-veiled boredom, but as it's to enquire about the food on offer in the café, I sense it only makes the security person feel even more disillusioned with their life. Perhaps their pace has slowed too much. I fear one day my wife, if told there are no scones on offer, could lose it completely and trash the exhibits in a wild rage whilst I scuffle with the sweaty security guard, trying to calm things down, thankful that the children, in the gift shop, will be oblivious to the whole debacle.

Plans are great but it is the direction rather than the destination that is more important.

One of the phrases often repeated by NLP devotees is 'there is no failure only feedback'. This is true when we set a flexible and positive direction but resist a fixed positive destination.

In *Out of Our Minds*, Ken Robinson describes creativity as a process of successive approximations. This means new ideas do not usually arrive fully formed and finished. Ideas go through the four stages of preparation, incubation, illumination and verification. You may have noticed these four stages mirror the four suits of this little book. The four steps within creativity at its best is analogous to the four steps within planning at its best. Planning our future through a series of successive approximations allows us to have the best of both worlds. Those worlds are:

• setting challenging but realistic ambitions, and
• being flexible to adapt and develop new plans as a result of the changing world around us.

A great example of this process is physicist Richard Feynman describing how he developed an idea that led him to a Nobel prize. He saw a child drop a plate in a cafeteria; and noticed that the plate wobbled as it spun and he thought it looked as though the wobble was moving more slowly than the spinning plate. He played around with the equations of this process, just for fun. This eventually led him to a new understanding of the spin of an electron.

6

Walk This Way
Time: 10 mins

Activity: Set up a simple obstacle course and select two pairs of volunteers. The first pair decides on roles — one guide and one player. The player, who can talk, has to walk backwards avoiding the obstacles to reach the end of the course, guided only by the instructions of the guide who can only say yes or no. The whole group can take the role of guide. Choose safe obstacles, including sheets of paper, cuddly toys, a few chairs etc. It doesn't need to resemble the set from Jim Henson's *Labyrinth*. The second pair repeats the activity but the player faces forward. This may seem a lot of effort to make a simple point, but ask the group how many have a plan detailing where they're going, with an awareness of the obstacles ahead with a guide to help them along the way, and most will respond negatively. An alternative is to blindfold the first player, as they may be tempted to cheat while walking backwards. You can also have two players instead of one, joined by a scarf or similar item.

Learning Point: It's easier when we know where we're going!

This may seem obvious but how many of us know where we want to be in three, five or ten years time?

Preparation: You need a room in which you can set up a basic obstacle course.

6

7 of Clubs: A Little Time

The learning point of this activity is to take time to consider all of our options. By reflecting on the options ahead of us we are more likely to make the best choice. This process may also help reveal additional opportunities.

How many triangles are there? (Answer 24).

What's the minimum number of pencils you can remove to leave two squares? (Remove the two shaded pencils).

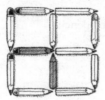

Learn it before the session.

Place six pencils together in such a way that they all touch each other.

The more competitive group members tend to enjoy these activities. Encourage and provide clues to ensure all groups solve the problems.

Timing is important. My dad was a Robbie Williams impersonator in the 1970s; he had a great act but got no work! Apologies for that joke: I'll try harder from now on.

7

A Little Time
Time: 2–5 mins

Activity: Ask, 'How many triangles can you see?' (Answer: 24).

Ask, 'What's the least number of pencils you can remove to leave two squares?' (Remove the two shaded pencils).

Ask, 'Can you place six pencils together so they all touch each other?'

Learning Point: More time to think things through often means we get better results. Sharing challenges with others can lead to better results.

In work, this is the usual way, not only sitting in exam conditions.

Preparation: A box of pencils.

7

8 of Clubs: SMART

The SMART approach is a great way to assess and improve goals.

S Specific to you
M Measurable (so you know when you've achieved the goal)
A Achievable (not too hard or too easy)
R Realistic
T Timed (you set a deadline to make sure you achieve your goal)

An interesting addition is to change the 'R' to right direction, which applies the 'outcome frame' approach used in NLP, as opposed to the 'blame frame' (see below).

Ask small groups to work on making a goal 'SMART' – either a personal one related to a course or career decision, or a group challenge such as raising money for charity.

The right direction ('outcome frame') requires the following questions:

• What's the best that could happen?
• How would you feel if it did?
• What skills, knowledge, resources do you have, or could access, to help you get it?
• What is the result you would like to achieve?
• Which people could help?

The 'blame frame' questions include:

• What's the worst that could happen?
• How would you feel if this happened?
• Who is to blame?
• How long has this been a problem?

If you ask groups to discuss an issue, first using 'blame frame' then dealing with the same question using 'outcome frame' questions, they will notice a big difference. A sample statement could be, 'Young people are not achieving their full potential'.

Clubs - Have a Plan

8
SMART
Time: 15 mins

Activity: Students make a goal SMART.

They can either work on their own, in pairs, or you could do this as a group activity.

Topics can be general and impersonal — 'Make Sunderland AFC the best football team in the world,' for instance.

Or personal — 'Be my best'.

Learning Point: SMART objectives are better than vague ideas.

Preparation: None.

8

9 of Clubs: The Miracle Question

Asking a great question can help someone see themselves differently: preferably at their best. These can be described as 'miracle questions'. The original miracle question goes along the following lines: 'If you woke up tomorrow and a miracle happened that meant everything was as you wanted it to be, what would be different?'

In NLP, 'dissociation' is commonly used for this purpose. Dissociation is asking someone to step out of their own shoes to see themselves from the position of an observer. For example, if you need to talk to a student about unacceptable behaviour, you could ask, 'What would you do if you were me, to make sure your behaviour improved?' This question can provide a useful insight into the thinking behind the behaviour of the student. I once asked my son, 'What punishment would you give to you, if you were me?' He thought about it for a few seconds (dissociating) and suggested it would be no pocket money, because he didn't mind being sent to his bedroom. I thanked him and said I'd consider his punishment and get back to him.

The quickest way to dissociate someone is with a question. A few words that can make a world of difference. In *Expectation: The Very Brief Therapy Book*, Rubin Battino suggests that when all else fails some therapists will ask the client for the answer. Perhaps we should ask the client *before* all else fails. He offers 'The Miracle Question' as an approach.

Good questions will focus on things that:

Are really important to the student.

Require action by the student.

They will/can do (not what they won't/can't do).

Are specific,

Consider who, where and when rather than why.

Examples of 'miracle questions' include:

What would you do if you knew you couldn't fail?

What advice would you give to someone identical to you?

9

The Miracle Question
Time: 5-10 mins

Activity: Ask students questions such as:

- What would you do if you knew you couldn't fail?
- What advice would you give to someone identical to you?
- If you could be your best, how would your life turn out?

Learning Point: The direction in which we turn our attention and thoughts can determine the quality and usefulness of the answers we receive. Ask yourself questions using the miracle question rules for better answers.

Preparation: None.

9

10 of Clubs: Two Out of Three

This activity is based on group discussion, generally small groups followed by feedback to the whole group. You can spice it up by having gender-based groups to discover if there are different patterns of thought.

As the theme of this section is planning, you may like to ask, 'How would you plan for these things?'

We often use words like famous, happy, healthy, to describe what we want out of life, as if they are a product to be consumed. Most research tends to suggest it is the process not the product that brings satisfaction: life as a verb rather than a noun. In NLP, turning process words into nouns is called 'nominalisation'.

When someone says they want to be famous, we can use the word as a starting point to explore exactly what this means. Communication difficulties often occur when people assume they know what someone means, rather than clarifying the meaning. (This is explored further in Part Two.)

So we must be careful when asking people to commit to plans. They must be aware that the destination, though important, is not the goal itself. Plan for the future but live in the present. The idea of 'flow', described by Mihaly Csikszentmihalyi, draws similar conclusions. Peak flow is achieved when we're on the learning curve, not when we have reached the top, when our attention is directed toward realistic goals, not too hard or too easy. This is why watching TV, although the number one leisure time activity, does not satisfy us as much as many other activities. Flow at all logical levels results in peak satisfaction. The four sections in this book have arrows drawn between them because it is the continuous movement around the four parts that makes us grow into the best we can be. We don't just go round once, we keep going and growing with lots of extra free goes!

10

Two Out of Three
Time: 5-8 mins

Activity: If you could be just one of the following, which would you choose?

To be:

- Famous.
- Rich.
- Wise.
- Happy.
- Beautiful.
- Healthy.

Discuss in groups.

Learning Point: Ask how can you plan for these?

Make them *SMART* (*8 of Clubs*).

Preparation: You could prepare cards for each group.

Alternatively, use pictures of people famous for the description.

10

Jack of Clubs: I Predict a ...

Interestingly, it is predicted that 90% of the jobs 5-year-olds will be doing when they leave education have yet to be invented. Think back 10 or 20 years – which jobs did not exist? They would include anything to do with mobile phones, satellite TV, using newly invented equipment in hospitals to treat and diagnose illnesses, etc. What jobs might exist in the future? Apparently there are now more mobile phones in the UK than there are people. A collection of these types of facts can form the basis of an interesting discussion.

The purpose is to be aware of such trends so that our plans are as well researched as possible. Trends are only a guide, so we must choose course and career options based on an understanding of our own innate qualities, as these can be the foundation of a long and successful career.

However, I've spoken to many groups of teenagers and I've often followed other speakers who have been from industry or business and described as 'experts' by teaching staff keen to excite the students as they settle down and prepare to absorb wisdom from the cutting edge. Often their message is based on the following ideas.

- The world is changing, the pace of change ever faster.
- The world of business is tough and it's survival of the fittest.
- To compete with China/India YOU must become highly qualified, skilled, flexible, entrepreneurial, driven, do what you're told and be prepared to break the rules. Oh, and dress smartly.

I've never quite been comfortable with that message even when it's delivered with wit and enthusiasm, though more often it is delivered in a patronising and dull drizzle over the course of around 50 PowerPoint slides. Personally, I've never found the world of business to be tougher than most secondary school playgrounds. That's not my main problem with the message. Point a finger at little

Johnny and say, 'You must compete with China and India', and they're likely to think, 'What, me on my own? Take on China and India?!' They'll be scared and rightly so. Wouldn't you be? I think we need to send people into the world self aware and confident of their own skills, purpose and abilities so they can be their best.

Britain does really well in many industries, particularly those requiring creativity. I heard the former Director of the CBI, Lord (Digby) Jones, eloquently describe a path for Britain to ensure success. He countered the argument by those bemoaning the collapse of manufacturing in the UK (so we may as well give up) by looking at what happens to the £10 you pay for a Harry Potter figure bought from Argos. Yes, it's made in China and they receive around £1 to make it and ship it here. But the rest of the money, the majority, goes to the British designers, advertisers, marketing people, Argos and the staff working there, Warner Brothers, and JK Rowling's royalty. As a country, we need to look at our strengths to ensure we are successful and not look at what we can't do. We require the same approach as individuals if we are to be successful.

Predicting the future? Here are some more discussion point quotes:

We don't like their sound, and guitar music is on the way out

Decca Records reject the Beatles in 1962

There is no reason in the world anyone would want a computer in their home. No reason.

Ken Olsen, Chairman, DEC, 1977

The best way to predict the future is to invent it.

Alan Kay

Another follow-on activity is to ask students to think of a job and then its opposite, like 'undertaker' and 'midwife'.

The national obsession is predicting the weather. Apparently, if you predict that tomorrow will be much the same as today you'll be right two out of every three days. Saves time watching the weather forecast.

I Predict a ... J
Time: 5 mins

Activity: (1) Ask students to rank the job areas on the list with those increasing most first:

- Computing and IT.
- Health Services.
- Transportation services.
- Residential care of the elderly.
- Leisure/Recreation services.

(They are ranked as they are listed above and are all increasing.)

Source: Do What You Are, Paul Tieger

(2) A follow-on activity is to ask students for their predictions. What jobs, inventions, etc, do they foresee?

(3) Use sample predictions of the future.

Learning Point: Be aware of trends so our plans are as well researched as possible. But trends are only a guide so we must choose course and career options based on understanding our own strengths and talents, as these are with us for life.

Preparation: None.

J

Queen of Clubs: Timeline

We are the biggest influence on our own future. Yes, other people and events will have an impact but not as much as we have. We can take control over our own lives if we really go for it, using all the new information we have gathered about self-belief, our strengths, our ability to plan and the attitude of success.

Encourage students to consider the obstacles they may have to overcome and how they feel about each. What resources (skills, attitudes, friends, knowledge) do they currently have and what can they do to plug any gaps? I usually ask people to work in pairs and encourage each other to think big when charting their life above the line. Obviously, some people will be guarded and others very open, so this has to be handled sensitively. Many achievers describe a specific moment when they just decided to follow their dream. For the comedian Jimmy Carr it was after his mum died. In a newspaper interview, he said, 'It makes you go, right, I'm going to go to work now and do something with myself and I'm going to have a bit more fun. I'm going to have a dessert. I'm going to live a life.'

In NLP, this activity is often done in physical space rather than on a sheet of paper, and often with amazing and revealing results. This is a watered-down version but it can still produce very positive outcomes.

Timeline
Time: 5–15 mins

Activity: Each person draws a diagonal line across a sheet of A4 paper and writes 'born' and 'die' at each end. They fill in the important events on their line up until now and then fill in their future, branching off from now in two ways — one below the line, if they continue as they are now, and then above the line if they really go for it, using all the new information they have about self belief, their strengths and ability to plan, the attitude of success. They can highlight obstacles to overcome and how they feel about each. I ask people to work in pairs.

Learning Point: Successful people plan their future success.

We have more control of our future than we think.

Preparation: None.

King of Clubs: Marge or Homer

There are two opposing approaches to planning. Some people like to plan, decide, work on one project until it is completed and then move to the next subject on their list. Others prefer to be more flexible, adopting a 'go with the flow' kind of approach, starting lots of different projects without too much concern for deadlines. In other words: Marge or Homer Simpson. There are advantages and disadvantages to both. The real skill is to know which is best for the situation you face. As it's usually impossible to know this without hindsight, it's best to consider how you can apply the best of both approaches. Think through the situation first using one mindset, then repeat using the other. Useful insights usually result. Sample questions can include:

- How to find the person you're going to marry.
- How to choose a course or a job.

These two approaches are referred to as 'meta-programs' in NLP, hard-wired ways of thinking that impact on our behaviour. Options (Homer) or procedures (Marge). These two different attitudes to life are considered important parts of personality and have a big impact in schools.

Students who use a procedure approach tend to do well at school because they are organised and structured in their work. They usually stick to deadlines. Students who use an options approach could be at a disadvantage at school because they prefer variety and an unstructured environment. Schools, and indeed most large organisations, use a procedures approach. You can explore the advantages and disadvantages of each approach. For more details see my book, *The Buzz*. If you would like to see how other meta-programs fundamentally influence our behaviour, I recommend the excellent work by Shelle Rose-Charvet, summarised in her book *Words That Change Minds*.

K Marge or Homer
Time: 10 mins

♣

Activity: Ask students to stand on one side of the room or the other depending upon which statement they prefer: *'I like to get things sorted and finished before I play'* or *'I can play anytime'*. Peer pressure (when we're young) can influence more people to join the latter group but statistically there should be an equal split. You can explore the advantages and disadvantages of each approach.

Learning Point: The world generally favours the Marge group. School and business tend to set deadlines, and rewards those that meet these requirements.

Preparation: You need enough space to allow students to stand comfortably at opposing sides of the room. When they are ready, make sure you can put across a few meaningful points! For example: school and work favours the 'Marge' approach; it's cooler to have the 'Homer' approach; peer pressure often makes people say they're like Homer, whereas in the general population the split should be half and half; we're all susceptible to peer pressure.

K

SPADES

SPADES

Believe in Yourself

Know Your Strengths

Have a Plan

Go For It

Go For It

Happy the man, happy he alone,
He who can call the day his own.
He who can look back with pride and say,
Tomorrow do thy worst for I have lived today.

Henry Fielding, from his novel, *Tom Jones*

Whether we go for it or not is mostly determined by the state we're in at the time. Our brains assess things really quickly. We can then wait years mulling over what to do next when really deep down we know what to do. Most learning happens really quickly. This may be counter-intuitive, but it's true. 'It is in our moments of decision that our destinies are shaped,' says US motivation guru Anthony Robbins.

Take a phobia, for example. Most phobias are learned really quickly, in seconds. Many people who are scared of spiders had an older brother who threw a spider at them when they were young. They experienced fear and lack of control and in that moment the fear of spiders was burned into the wiring of their brain. It can stay for a lifetime. Adults can shake and sweat simply on hearing the word 'spider' 30 years after their learning experience. Wow! Brothers have a lot to answer for. Teachers have the same power. Most people who are scared of singing, drawing, maths etc learned this at school in one go.

I had a fear of singing for 20 years. In Year 7 I sat with the rest of the class in a music lesson. The teacher sat at the front tucked in by her piano and announced she was going to play a note and in turn we would stand up and sing the note. As the others took their turns, I became more and more anxious. By the time she called my name and played a note I could hardly stand up for shaking, never mind sing. I made some sort of noise and she turned to me wagging her finger, and said, 'Hodgson, that was pathetic. You can't sing.' To her credit, she taught me something quickly.

Unfortunately, and I'm a little uncomfortable as I type this because I remember the humiliation as if I'm back in the room with her bony finger pointing at me, it was not a positive learning experience. I didn't know anything about 'state dependent memory' and 'learning theory' whilst in this music lesson, but my brain did. It knew how to learn and remember effectively.

Twenty years later, whilst on an NLP course, someone helped me change this memory. Having never sung a note whilst anyone was around over those 20 years, I decided to show that woman what I was made of and I sang in front of 120 people. And they didn't run out of the room screaming with blood pouring out of their ears. We do learn quickly when we're scared but there should be no place for this type of learning in schools. Many people believe they can't sing or can't draw or can't do maths or sport after similar experiences at school.

If we learn when feeling bad we learn to avoid the subject, object or goal. If we learn whilst feeling good we tend to be drawn toward the subject, object or goal. There is a better way to learn and we'll explore it in this section. The only exception to the rule is the case of the judge in the United States who punished teenagers for playing their thumpy thumpy music (sorry, don't know the proper name, my interest in pop music has waned since the mid-1980s) too loudly by making each boy listen to two hours of Barry Manilow belting out his classic hits. Apparently it was a more effective deterrent than any previous punishments. Politicians take note – this could be cheaper than ASBOs.

We don't 'go for it' when we procrastinate, fear change or don't know how to, so we'll deal with all three in this section. We'll explore 'go for it' in the contexts of school, learning and life in general.

A ship in harbour is safe, but that is not what ships are built for.

William Shed

 Spades – Go For It

Those who try to do something and fail are infinitely better than those who try to do nothing and succeed.

Anon

There is only the moment. The now. Only what you are experiencing at this second is real. This does not mean you live for the moment. It means you live in the moment.

Leo Buscaglia

These quotes complement the final activity of this book, The Splash Zone.

143

Ace of Spades: Go For It State

Think of and describe the moods you were in when you did your very best. Compare your feelings within your group. The best states are positive, go for it, in the zone, that sort of thing, regardless of whether it's for sporting or personal success.

We achieve our best when we're in positive states. We may not always get the result we want but we'll have done our best and we can do no more than that.

This activity underpins the theme of this book, namely inspiration. It follows the other suits.

Although you don't need props, I received interesting feedback from a careers adviser using this activity. She bought a number of gingerbread men and piping icing, so each mood could be represented on to a biscuit. A means of learning that also creates a tasty snack has to be a great idea.

A great example of people preferring to stick with what they know can be found in the list of items the British take on holiday with them whey they travel abroad. This can be a good guessing game with a group. What do you think? What do you take abroad?

The top five in the survey I read were:

- Tea bags.
- Chocolate bars.
- Jars of Marmite.
- Packets of biscuits.
- Tins of beans.

A

Go For It State
Time: 5-10 mins

Activity: Ask students to compare how they feel when they're at their best and at their worst. Provide examples of sporting performance, interviews, exams, Christmas morning, birthdays etc.

Learning Point: We tend to perform well when in a positive state such as go for it or relaxed, and badly when we're nervous.

Preparation: None.

A

2 of Spades: Time Bandits

We all have our favourite excuses and distractions. If only I'd been taller, thinner, better looking, younger, older, had less commitments, richer, luckier, etc. One of the best I heard was a 16-year-old boy blaming his lack of academic success on the fact his birthday was late in the school year. OK, this could have been a factor in his early years, but he'd surely had enough time to make up for it by the time he'd reached 16.

Successful people tend to be busy. They get involved with activities that they enjoy or are leading to a particular favourable outcome. I like the saying, 'If you want something doing, ask a busy person.'

Many entrepreneurs, such as Duncan Bannatyne, identify their attitude to time bandits as crucial to their success. Their 'go for it' attitude serves them well. Without this, all the talent and intelligence young people possess is wasted.

You can be specific and deal with time bandits around school success or life in general or to the *Wheel of Life* (2 of Clubs). A logical follow-on activity is *6 of Spades*, which deals with motivation.

2 Time Bandits

Time: 5 mins

Activity: What are your time bandits?

What excuses do you regularly use to stop you from going for things?

They can be limiting beliefs about ourselves or the opportunities available; we can blame other people; we can distract ourselves with TV, YouTube and all manner of things.

You can split this activity into 'time bandits' around school success and life in general or to the *Wheel of Life* (2 *of Clubs*).

This can work well as an activity in small groups or pairs followed up by a general discussion, including finding out which are the most common within the group as a whole. Students could offer solutions to each other.

Learning Point: Procrastination, distraction, sloth, excuses et al prevent us from achieving our best.

A great way to overcome these is to have a goal in mind, as described in *6 of Spades*.

Preparation: None.

2

3 of Spades: Shoe Swap

This is a simple and effective activity.

The learning points are:

- We all have habits.
- We like to stick with what we know.
- We can only learn and grow by exploring and experiencing alternatives.

The experience of change is rarely as bad as the thought of change

We all like to have control in our lives and we can only have control if we have choice. Choice exists if we have options. To create more options we must try new things. Only by trying something new can we learn new knowledge, skills, attitudes and beliefs.

99% of what we worry about never happens yet we worry and worry. What a horrible way to go through life. What a horrible thing to do to your colon.

Leo Buscaglia

The shoe swap exercise also shows us that some of our habits are good for us, such as putting our shoes on the right feet. When I originally developed this activity I asked people to swap shoes with a partner. Although very amusing, watching men tottering around in high heels, it proved too gross for the more hygiene conscious in the group, especially in summer months when some teenagers' trainers could probably walk on their own.

3

Shoe Swap
Time: 5 mins

Activity: Swap your shoes over and walk in them around the room you're in. What does it feel like?

Learning Point: We get into habits — some good, some not — without realising it. Which habits or beliefs do you have that are useful/or not useful?

Preparation: Check you're wearing a clean pair of socks if you join in.

3

4 of Spades: Sign Your Name

This is a version of a well-known activity. It makes the same points as the previous activity but with a bonus learning point. If you ask students to sign their names with their 'other' hand ten times, they'll discover that they'll improve with practice. When we give up on things we stop getting better. It's the first few attempts that are hardest but when approached with a sense of fun and enjoyment, the learning curve is steep, which means we improve more quickly.

If students do not have a pen or pencil and paper, this 'fold your arms' activity is a good alternative: ask them to fold their arms and notice which arm is on top. Then ask them to fold their arms with the other hand on top. They'll notice it feels comfortable first time and awkward the second time.

Many of our habits and beliefs are useful to us. They become second nature, allowing more time to think about other stuff. Habits like ironing, putting on trousers and eating become things we can do with little or no thought. Though all three at once would probably present a challenge to most people, with the possible exception of parents with young children to get to school and jobs to go to ...

Blinking is a great example of useful automatic behaviour. We only think about blinking when our attention is drawn to the subject. Now you'll be aware of your blinking, especially if I challenge you not to blink! It's the same with nits. I've noticed that if I ever mention my children had head lice, people will start and scratch their heads. I wonder if your head is itching now? The chances of catching head lice from this book must be remote.

We often forget that we inhabit our habits. We delude ourselves that we have no choice. Yet we can and do change. Our brains never lose the capacity to change and grow. Our bones may stop growing but our cartilage never does. This is why our nose and ears grow throughout our lives and explains why, in old age, men and woman look similar.

4

Sign Your Name
Time: 2-5 mins

Activity: Ask students to sign their names, like they'd do if asked for their autograph.

Then sign it again using the other hand.

Learning Point: It's much harder second time.

We do all sorts of things as habits, some useful some not.

Ask which beliefs and habits they have that are useful and which are not?

Ask students to sign their name with their wrong hand 10 times and they'll notice they improve.

Practise, and we get better.

Preparation: Paper and pen per student.

4

5 of Spades: Sit Down

Here's another activity which illustrates our reluctance to change. Ask a group to stand up and sit in another seat – a sort of musical chairs but with enough chairs for everyone, an extreme example of non-competitive sport at its best or worst, depending on whether you read the *Guardian* or *Daily Mail*. When they sit down they'll feel uncomfortable at first but start to relax as they grow familiar with their environment. This process replicates, in a small but effective way, many experiences they will face of dealing with change in real life: starting a new school year, a new job, meeting new people.

This activity is often greeted with sighs and annoyance. I suppose this just illustrates the fact that we don't like change.

The fear of change nullifies our capacity to learn and grow. Some people spend a lifetime stuck in jobs or relationships that stifle their potential. Education is the best environment to nurture the attitude of success; a joy of learning about ourselves and the world around us. (My head still feels itchy does yours?)

5

Sit Down
Time: 2–5 mins

Activity: Ask students to stand up and then go and sit in another seat.

Learning Point: We like our comfort zones.

We distrust change.

We often stick with habits that are limiting.

Preparation: None.

5

6 of Spades: How to Have a Goal in Mind

Ask a group, 'what motivates you to ... come to school or college? (or just about anything or anywhere). You'll find that the responses can be quite predictable.

The four most common are:

- To avoid being told off my mum.
- To avoid a job I wouldn't like.
- To gain a good job or qualification.
- To be with friends and socialise.

The first two are examples of 'away from' motivation. This is when we are motivated by the thought of avoiding something bad. Companies selling insurance use this form of motivation to persuade us to buy, to avoid the hassle, distress, pain, etc, of floods and accidents. When we think of the example we feel bad and so act to avoid feeling bad.

These last two are examples of 'toward' motivation. This is when we are motivated by the thought of having, gaining or achieving something good. We feel good about having something good immediately, such as chocolate, or longer term, a healthy and attractive body if we diet, or a great job if we do well at school.

We access these feelings in all three major representational systems (visual, auditory and kinaesthetic – more in *3 of Hearts* and *10 of Spades*). Interestingly, people doing well at school tend to have two experiences of 'toward' motivation – feeling good about the short-term benefit of school, such as being with friends, and feeling good about their long-term, great career if they work hard. And they have one 'away from' experience – avoiding a bad job – that helps them keep it real.

I've noticed similar patterns in many strongly motivated individuals, including athletes and business achievers. I asked one keen swimmer what she thought of when she wakes. It transpired she pictures movie clips of episodes in her life in her head. First she imagines winning a gold medal at the Olympics, and she said, 'I can feel them put the medal around my neck, hear the national anthem and I can feel the weight of it.' As she said this she got goose bumps on her arms. Wow, I thought, she is really motivated and using V, A and K. She also said she thought that if she missed just one training session it could add a tenth of a second to her time in the final, which could be the difference between gold and fourth. She then said she imagined being back up on the podium looking out to her mum and dad in the crowd and she could see how proud they were and how much they loved her and she felt love for them as they had sacrificed so much to help her achieve her aims.

Never mind the swimmer being motivated, I was welling up myself. The swimmer does what so many people do who are strongly motivated: they access three memories, of which two are toward motivation and one is away from. Together they provide a propulsion that whisks them along to act. If teachers could help students build these kind of motivational strategies, the kids would be waiting at the school gates at five in the morning, shouting, 'Let us in, let us in, we want maths!'

Please note, we may be strongly motivated in some areas of our lives and not in others; for example, some young people are strongly motivated in a chosen sport but not about school in general. I've noticed people not doing well at school have mostly 'away from' motivation when thinking about school. They attend to avoid being punished by parents or others. Thus, they don't feel bad whilst at school, but they don't feel good. Feeling not bad, but not good does not create a student with a positive and motivated state when it comes to their learning. If they attend school to socialise with their peers, this is not related to the curriculum. No wonder teachers struggle to engage, motivate and inspire with a curriculum that the student has not attached to a 'toward' motivation outcome. No wonder these students are bored by the curriculum. Some schools are learning to tackle this head on with an alternative curriculum that is linked to positive, 'toward' motivation feelings. Another idea is to take students to visit universities, or potential employers, to make the curriculum real and relevant to the day-to-day study they undertake upon their return. As a careers adviser and NLP practitioner I'm used to exploring and changing these motivational experiences, so that people can discover ways to motivate themselves that are appropriate to their own ambitions.

Often, I'm met in schools by teachers who tell me that today I'll be working with a group of unmotivated students. There *are* no unmotivated students. My teenage son spends more time doing his hair than doing his homework. He may not be motivated by homework but he is by other things. When you understand how someone does motivation in their own head you can really start to influence them. If you just try and impose your own way of motivation onto others, it would be like trying to persuade Boris Johnson and John Prescott to vote for each other.

Entrepreneur John Elliot, speaking on *The Secret Millionaire*, said, 'One of my main regrets was leaving school at fifteen, it should have been thirteen.' His motivation for school was low but he *was* motivated to set up his own business, Ebac, now worth around £60 million.

And if you also make people feel bad whilst demanding they learn, well, you should go and sit at the naughty step or be sent to your room without supper. When you ask a teacher what they do, those that say they teach children are nearer than those that say they teach maths, science or whatever subject.

6

How to Have a Goal in Mind
Time: 10 mins

Activity: Ask students what motivates them to come to school.

Take answers and explore how they experience in V, A and K.

For example 'I picture myself in a great job' (V), 'hear family saying well done' (A) and, 'feel warm and confident/proud' (K).

(If the K is good it's 'toward' motivation and if it's bad it's 'away from' motivation.

For example, 'I picture myself being told off by my mum' (V) and, 'her voice telling me off' (A) and, 'feel bad' (K).

Distinguish between the two and compare to a swimmer's motivational strategy.

Do not judge anyone's thinking. The thing to ask is, does their thinking help them achieve their best?

Learning Point: We can understand how we motivate ourselves in different areas of our lives and assess the effectiveness. If it's not effective we can change our thinking.

Preparation: Have a good read of this activity and the supporting notes. Also have a look at the NLP in Part Two. This can be a brilliant activity.

6

7 of Spades: Thank You For the Music

There are nine million bicycles in Beijing. Now I don't know if this is a fact or if it was made up on the spot by singer/songwriter Katie Melua. Song lyrics stick in our head and this makes them an entertaining way to learn and remember information. Unconvinced? I challenge you not to be singing by the time you reach the end of this word – 'supercalifragilisticexpialidocious'. Rhymes can be as equally effective if repeated enough. 'Mary had a little lamb, its …' Did you say the next line? It's hard not to.

I can remember catchphrases from TV commercials of more than 25 years ago … and an enjoyable evening's entertainment it can make if I'm with friends of a similar age.

This technique is fine for remembering information but not for understanding the content. Nursery rhymes are good examples. We remember the words:

Mary, Mary, Quite contrary,
How does your garden grow?
With silver bells and cockle shells, etc

But we don't always remember the meaning – apparently this rhyme is about Queen Mary torturing people, and silver bells are a sort of thumbscrew. I don't even want to think about what a cockleshell is …

Spades – Go For It

7

Thank You For the Music
Time: 5–10 mins

Activity: Challenge the group to put some facts they need to remember from a subject into the form of a song, rap or rhyme. The results can be genuinely hilarious.

Alternatively prepare something from your own subject. I use one about the formation of oxbow lakes to the tune of *Girlfriend in a Coma* by The Smiths.

Learning Point: Music and rhythm are natural ways to express words.

They can be an effective way to remember dry and abstract information.

Preparation: None.

7

8 of Spades: Take a Break

There are many books and websites offering revision tips. I tend to be disappointed, as they mostly state the obvious – take breaks, do a revision timetable, drink plenty of water, etc. We all have to hear this stuff for a first time but I'd like to pass on a couple of ways to relax during exams and tests that are less well known.

If stress or panic grips during an exam, tap the centre of your forehead three times with the three middle fingers of your hand, fingers pointing down to the floor. Repeat if needed. I'm told this stimulates activity in a part of the brain that helps us focus. This may be true or not, but it seems to work. Even if it is purely a distraction, if it works I'm happy to use it. My son tried it during a SAT test and his teacher asked him what he was doing. Still, he says it worked for him. I wouldn't recommend it, though, during a driving test as it obstructs vision, but while sitting at a desk it is relatively harmless. NLP is full of distractions of this sort to encourage people to change state. We also learn and remember better when relaxed.

Another example is the buttock clench. I'm told it is impossible to be nervous if you clench your buttocks tightly and hold the position for three seconds, then relax for three seconds and repeat. Go on, try it now, nobody is watching!

Asking the group to draw a circle, square and triangle simultaneously with both hands also seems to help relaxation and put a smile on the face, in a similar way to the tongue twister activity (*Joker Card*).

8

Take a Break
Time: 2–5 mins

Activity: Relax during times of stress by tapping your forehead or doing the buttock clench.

If stressed during an exam, tap the centre of your forehead three times with the three middle fingers of your hand, fingers pointing down to the floor. Repeat if needed. Then turn your attention back to the exam/test.

You could also attempt the buttock clench! While seated, clench your buttocks tightly and hold for three seconds, then relax for three seconds and repeat. I'm told we can't be nervous whilst doing this. This may be simply because most people laugh or can't believe what they're doing.

Learning Point: We perform below our full potential when we're nervous.

Learning techniques that reduce or remove nerves helps us perform at our best.

Preparation: None.

8

9 of Spades: Relax

An entertaining and instructional way to prove that some people don't perform or remember well when they are really nervous is to show some sample wrong answers given by contestants on quiz shows such as *Who Wants to Be a Millionaire?*, *Family Fortunes* or *The Weakest Link* (widely available on the internet/YouTube). They graphically illustrate how nerves can destroy memory.

The fear visible on some of the contestants' faces when failing to correctly answer questions that could win them a holiday or a fridge-freezer is frightening. We won't do well in exams if we follow their example.

I once interviewed someone for a job who was shaking at the beginning of the interview and she really struggled to answer the first question, which was, 'You must be Sharon?' Surely that's not going to feature in a book of tough interview questions?

A teacher told me he gave out exam howlers to help his students prepare for exams. I'm not sure I would advocate that myself: I'm not trying to make students feel stupid here! I'm hinting that their performance will be better if they're in an appropriate state during an exam, interview, first date etc. The words we use are crucial. In the book *Yes! 50 Secrets from the Science of Persuasion*, there is a good example from the hotel industry. Many hotels have introduced signs in rooms requesting that occupants re-use towels to save on laundry and the environment. But by changing a few words and saying that the majority of guests recycle their towels at some point during their stay, they experienced a 26% increase in the amount of recycling in those rooms compared to the other rooms. This utilizes the 'social proof' concept that we're more inclined to follow the example of other people. This, and the other 'rules of influence' outlined in this excellent book, should be studied and applied by teachers and schools.

9

Relax
Time: 3-5 mins

Activity: Show the group examples of wrong answers given on TV quiz shows such as *Family Fortunes, Who Wants to Be a Millionaire* etc,

Learning Point: We are at our best when relaxed and focused.

We are at our worst when nervous.

Preparation: Wrong answers from the Internet.

9

10 of Spades: Sucking Lemons

We access states – 'moods' – when V, A and K are all experienced.

If someone is asked to recall the state they were in during their first kiss they will probably picture the person they kissed or where it took place, hear stuff that was said, and feel the feelings they had of nerves/satisfaction/pleasure/alarm/vague stirrings, or whatever. We're always running little movies in our heads.

These states build with what NLP calls 'submodalities'. These are the size, place, colour of the pictures; the volume, source, intensity of the sounds we hear, and the speed, temperature and direction of the feelings we experience.

This activity, sucking lemons, allows you to demonstrate the power of submodalities. After one demo, someone in the audience asked me if I'd meant to say 'lemons' because I'd actually said 'melons'. Mistakes are often more useful than getting it right every time.

What a good mistake I'd made. The same letters in a slightly different order made a huge difference to the audience. And this is what teachers can do so well: use words to make a huge difference with their audience. Use the opposite of sarcasm (heavy words are so lightly thrown). Use words to create strong positive states with vivid pictures, sounds, tastes and feelings to motivate and inspire.

A teacher friend was advised, on a Using NLP in Teaching course, to employ this approach. She told me she'd said to a girl in her class, who was often distracted and chatty: 'You know, Sarah, when I look at you I see a really bright girl with loads of potential, who is choosing to mess about, instead of getting on with her work. Come on Sarah, you can do this.' She'd never praised the girl before and she said the girl's eyes welled up with tears and their relationship changed from that moment. We can inspire when we fire all three main systems together, and if we throw in some of the other 15 or so senses whilst in a positive state, we will be in flow, at our best, and will remember everything vividly.

The lemon activity is simple but illustrates the importance of VAK. Students can then use this in their own learning and revision.

10

Sucking Lemons
Time: 3–5 mins

Activity: One of the classic ways to demonstrate a principle of NLP is lemon tasting. Act out this activity whilst you describe it. Ask students to hold out one hand, and cup it.

Tell them to imagine holding a lemon. Feel the weight of it. Observe the bright yellow skin. Feel the dimpled and waxy skin in your fingers. As you smell it, imagine it cut into quarters and with your other hand pick up one of the quarters and place it in your mouth. Feel the lemon juice on your tongue and feel it trickle down the back of your throat.

Learning Point: If students play along, their mouths should be watering, illustrating the mind-body link and that experience is processed by visual means (picturing a lemon), auditory (listening to the description), and kinaesthetic (feeling the juice in our mouth and pulling a sucking-lemons face). We can learn and remember things using these three systems.

Preparation: None.

10

Jack of Spades: Teach Someone Else

There is a saying that you don't really understand something fully until you have to teach it. Once you've taught something a few times you really know it. This approach is under-used in education.

Various researchers, for example as described in *The Teacher's Toolkit*, by Paul Ginnis, suggest we remember 90–95% of what we teach to others, and as little as 5% of what we're made to listen to. I sometimes teach a card trick to someone at the beginning of a session, before the whole group has arrived, and ask them to demonstrate it and then teach it to someone else. There's a number of these in *Could It Be Magic?* in Part Two.

Mentoring and using peers to teach some aspects of the curriculum is spreading in many schools and it benefits everyone. It replicates the learning process before formal education as we know it today became commonplace. In the past, a child was educated by the whole village, not one adult.

J

Teach Someone Else
Time: 5-10 mins

Activity: Teach a student a magic trick/illusion from *Could It Be Magic?* in Part Two.

Ask them to show the group then teach the group.

Learning Point: We really understand something when we teach or demonstrate it to others, rather than simply recalling information. Use this during revision. Go and explain something to someone else. Not only does it give you a change of scenery and pace it will really help you understand the subject matter well as well as help you find out which bits you don't yet know.

Preparation: Choose a trick or game from *Could It Be Magic?* in Part Two.

J

Queen of Spades: Memory Technique

The world record holder for memory could recall the English-Chinese dictionary in both directions. He could remember all of the English words with their Chinese definition and all the Chinese words with their English definition. Wow! The illusionist Derren Brown studied memory techniques and describes those he finds most effective in his book *Trick of the Mind*. He used the techniques to help him remember cases for his Law degree. I pass on one of the techniques to students to demonstrate how easy and effective the method can be. It is the journey method, linking facts by placing them on a relevant and distinctive journey. It takes around five to 10 minutes to teach and I check at the end of a session a couple of hours later to show how effective it is.

I choose Oscar-winning films from 1990 to 2000. We start by asking everyone to imagine walking out of the cold or rain into the warmth of a new, glass-fronted cinema. I ask, 'What do we smell?' and someone will say popcorn, hot dogs or sick. I ask, 'What colour is the carpet?' They usually say red, occasionally blue. I say, 'Feel the red carpet underfoot and look to your left and see some black wolves dancing with some white lambs'. We then write up

Dances with Wolves (1990) and

Silence of the Lambs (1991).

We then go over to the ticket booth where Clint Eastwood is sitting, wearing his cowboy hat and looking really annoyed because he'd rather be in his film

The Unforgiven (1992).

Write it up. Then, instead of a ticket he gives us a list. Ask for the colour of the list. We're asked to give the list, *Schindler's List*, which smells of chocolate, to *Forrest Gump* who said life is like a box of chocolates. Write up

Schindler's List (1993), and

Forrest Gump (1994).

Now we take the list to Screen Five. This reminds us the next film is from 1995. At the entrance is Mel Gibson dressed in a kilt and he does a Scottish jig. I ask everyone to stand up and do a little Scottish jig; this is compulsory, to ensure we remember. The film is

Braveheart (1995).

Write it up. Next, we go into the cinema and settle down to watch the film and it's back in England with

The English Patient (1996),

travelling on the

Titanic (1997),

who is in love with Shakespeare

Shakespeare in Love (1998).

Write them up. The English patient in love with Shakespeare is going to America to meet a beauty, an

American Beauty (1999),

but will have to fight a gladiator when he gets there. Ask them to picture a gladiator waiting in America standing like the statue of Liberty. Write up

Gladiator (2000).

I also point out that the first letters of the six films spell out BETSAG and I show them where I've written the titles. I underline the letters using a different colour. Run through the whole thing again and they always remember this, even weeks later.

Other great books with more on this and other memory techniques are *How to Develop a Brilliant Memory Week by Week*, by Dominic O'Brien and *Success in the Creative Classroom*, co-authored by Independent Thinking associate, Roy Leighton. Remember to check out Roy's Memory Matrix based on the famous Ebbinghaus Curve of Forgetting (p 141).

1990 Dances with Wolves

1991 Silence of the Lambs

1992 The Unforgiven

1993 Shindler's List

1994 Forrest Gump

1995 Braveheart

1996 The English Patient

1997 Titanic

1998 Shakespeare in Love

1999 American Beauty

2000 Gladiator

The fact that groups of teenagers remember this sequence of films is more remarkable considering many will not have seen some of them.

As a follow-on activity assemble a group of 6 to 8 unrelated objects and challenge teams to memorise the objects using the same memory technique used to recall the Oscar winning films.

Alternatively challenge students to memorise something useful from a subject they study and share it with the group next time you meet.

Memory Technique
Time: 10 + 5 mins

Activity: Learning tricks:

Learn a list by making a familiar journey in your mind's eye.

Examples: your journey to school; around the room in which you learn the subject you'd like to remember; your house.

Make a story out of it.

This is how many great memory champions do it.

E.g. Oscar-winning films from 1990 to 2000.

Follow the script for this card, as it's too long to fit in here.

Test the memory of the group at a later point. You'll be amazed by how well they remember.

Learning Point: Great memory masters use this technique, the 'journey method'. It combines the three keys of memory: association, location and imagination.

Preparation: Somewhere to write up the films as they are recalled.

King of Spades: I've Changed My Mind

We've learned techniques to help us fix information into our memories. Now we'll look at a way to remove unhelpful things.

This activity requires a bit of confidence on your part and is best done when you have established good rapport and have most, if not all, on board your ship of happiness sailing to Success Harbour, to dock in the port of Go For It (in the Land of Tortured Metaphor). I've had feedback from teenagers that when they next meet the person they were thinking of in this activity they hear the Benny Hill tune in their heads and don't feel so bad. Sometimes groups even download the music to play back and remind themselves of this game.

In *Stumbling on Happiness*, Daniel Gilbert highlights a further reason why being in a positive state is so important. How we see our future depends on how we are in the present. People were asked if they were happy. Those asked when the weather was bad answered more negatively than those asked when the sun was shining. Interestingly, the respondents were themselves not aware of how their answer had been influenced. This concept, called 'prefeeling', means if we are feeling good (in classrooms for example) we don't just benefit in the present but it could also help us make better decisions about our future. Teachers out there, make a note of how powerful this is.

This activity is an excellent example of one of the cornerstones of NLP – 'reframing'. By changing the sub-modalities (VAK) of a memory we change our mood, our state. In this example, such a change is effected by the use of music. The music is then a trigger – an 'anchor' – ready to enjoy a better mood next time we meet the person in question.

There are similar versions of this game in the excellent book *NLP: The New Technology of Achievement*, by Steve Andreas and Charles Faulkner. There are other brilliant activities in the book that take you further, if you'd really like to go for it.

We often reframe our experiences with the benefit of time. You can be laughing about an experience, sharing it as a treasured anecdote at a dinner party, with tears of laughter rolling down your cheeks, but three years ago, when you were in the grip of the incident, the tears on your cheeks were of frustration, pain or anger.

1) Talk about someone who makes you feel sad ...

2) Repeat words exactly whilst dancing to up-tempo music ...

RESULT: SAME WORDS
DIFFERENT FEELINGS

Indeed, the expression 'I'll laugh about this in ten years time' is a typical example of this process. In fact, the next time someone says that to you simply ask them, 'Why wait that long?'

There was a funny story in the press recently suggesting all new visitors to Britain would be given a cup of tea on arrival to put them in a good mood – a very British way to attempt to influence the moods of all sorts of people.

K   I've Changed My Mind
Time: 10 mins

Activity: Ask students to work in pairs.

You need a sober and serious mood.

Ask them to share some information about someone who makes them feel bad when they think of them. Not someone in the room. Don't name them. Share three things about the person, something about what they look like (they're 6 ft tall with blond hair), something they say (they always say they're too busy and if they didn't work so hard nothing would get done) and how they make you feel (sad, cross with myself). Swap one piece of information at a time. The mood will be sober and downbeat. If some people start to laugh then stop, you're ready for the next bit.

Then say I'd like you to repeat the conversation you've just had word-for-word, or as near as you can remember. This time we'll do two things differently. One, we'll be standing up, and two, we'll be dancing to some music. Then get them to stand up before they think themselves out of it. Put on some loud, silly music such as the *Benny Hill* theme and remind them to repeat their conversation. If, like me, you dance badly it will help. Perhaps that's the only way you can dance. This time they should start to laugh and giggle. The mood will be different. Let the fun last a while. Thank them for joining in.

Learning Point: We can control our mood by changing the way we think (in this case using music and movement that is incongruous to the original negative state).

How cool is that!

Preparation: *Benny Hill* or similar soundtrack.

A great way to remember the four suits of activities is with the *Benny Hill* theme playing in your head. It makes us laugh and puts us in a positive state. If not, put down the *Guardian* and stop taking yourself so seriously. When we're young we naturally learn so much: language, counting, skills such as riding a bike and tying our shoe laces, because we access positive states regularly and we have a desire to learn. The preceding activities are designed to rec-reate these powerful ingredients.

These elements are as good for teachers as they are for students. They give more control to the student: control over their learning, behaviour, motivation and destination. There are two alternative ways that space probes can be constructed to ensure they reach the desired destination in deep space. In Passive Attitude Control the trajectory is programmed into the probes before they are launched and no further adjustments can be made during the mission. However, using Active Attitude Control, probes have the ability to adjust their course using various sensors (sensitivity to gravity, heat, etc) to ensure the target destination is reached. I believe in preparing students with Active Attitude Control using the activities in this book.

PART TWO

Bringing NLP into the Classroom

Bringing NLP into the Classroom

This section provides a more detailed background on NLP theory to help teachers/trainers better understand and deliver the activities in Part One even more effectively and confidently. There are also extra activities just for teachers for personal development and/or to form the basis of an Inset day (alongside activities from Part One). Suggestions on how to put together activities for different aims are also included.

The impact of NLP in education has not been extensively researched or coherently recorded. Tantalising glimpses have emerged from some researchers. In *Resolve, A New Model of Therapy*, Richard Bolstad describes the impact of an NLP Communication Skills course in a school. A six-month follow-up indicated an increase in student motivation (for students with a teacher attending the course compared to a control group). Another benefit was an improvement in student-to-student relationships: 64% never saw bullying behaviour in their classroom compared to 40% in the control group. Passing on NLP techniques directly to students through the activities in this book have had a direct and positive impact on many students in the areas of building confidence, self-esteem, a 'go for it' attitude and effective learning strategies. This section looks at how teachers can develop their own abilities to motivate and inspire. The results of research by Kate Benson, following an NLP training course for Primary and Secondary Teachers in County Durham, is described by the teachers themselves on the site www.meta4education.co.uk

An NLP machine

When people ask me what NLP is, I usually tell them about a group of women I used to work with. They shared an NLP machine, a small, silver box which produced a number that would determine how happy they would be for the whole week. You may be familiar with these machines. They're called 'scales' and the women were all in a 'fat-fighting' club. Every Monday they'd step on the machine and weigh themselves. If the number increased they'd jump off and remove heavy jewellery or clothes. if the number were still higher they'd often be sad for the rest of the week. If the number went down, they'd jump off the scales punching the air and high-fiving each other like professional footballers celebrating a goal. 'Yes,' they'd bark triumphantly, 'I've lost two ounces, get in!'

Now, the mood they enter happens very quickly. Almost as soon as they've seen the number, their brain and body completely enter the mood of joy, or agony.

Because it happens so quickly they do not notice what is happening. NLP is about understanding what happens in that split second, so that we can take control of the process and have a choice about how we react. That's why it can seem like magic, because having more choice about our state gives us more control over our behaviour, beliefs and values which, in turn, allows us to be our best – but only if we want to. Some people cling strongly to the belief that they have no choice about their moods or their lives. If this is the reality they've created then it is true – or it may as well be. Plato describes our view of the world as the shadows on a cave wall. They are shadows, not reality. This is an amazing insight and it frees us from unwanted behaviour, beliefs and values, and allows us to be our best. But only if we want to be.

For more, try: *Ace of Diamonds, 10 of Hearts, 2 of Clubs* and the *Joker Big Pants*.

Danger! Boiled sweets

I worked with a woman who clung to negative beliefs. People avoided conversation with her if at all possible. Another woman in our office had been to Beamish Museum, which depicts how life in the North East of England has been lived over the last 200 years or so. She had visited the old fashioned sweet shop where they make boiled sweets the traditional way. Pots of boiling sugary liquid are poured out on to metal plates in front of you. They set quickly and are given out free to grateful onlookers. Mmmm! Our colleague brought back to the office enough sweets for one each and as she handed them round we all took one. The negative woman I referred to earlier took hers and did the thing you sometimes do with a boiled sweet when, on your first suck, you accidentally swallow it. Your first reaction is normally shock and fear as you're not sure what's just happened. The second thought is usually 'Oh, perhaps I could bring it back up again coz that's twenty calories and I haven't had the benefit.' But it's usually too late and you have to let it go.

How long is it acceptable for you to be miserable after such an event? Most people would say a few seconds. The miserable woman I've referred to, and I'm not making this up, was still going on about it three months later. It got to the stage when someone in the office volunteered to go back to the museum to buy more sweets to stop this woman complaining. Someone else rightly pointed out that it wouldn't make any difference, she'd just find something else to moan about. This is true. We can allow our mood to be determined by events outside of our minds and bodies or not – just remember they are shadows on the cave wall.

> *Whenever I hear someone sigh that "life is hard", I'm always tempted to ask, "compared to what?"*
>
> *Sydney J. Harris, journalist*

For more try: 2 of Diamonds, King of Hearts, Ace of Clubs and 3 of Spades.

Memorable experiences

I heard Richard Bandler, co-founder of NLP, talking at an NLP seminar about his disappointment at the way some educators have misinterpreted his findings on VAK and learning. Teaching to just one system is wrong and dangerous. Would you say to a child

'You're a K learner so we'll poke out your eyes and ears with this pointy stick as you won't be needing them'. Pointless. We learn best when all three systems are fired up and we're in a positive state, such as feeling curious or excited.

I experienced an example of this whilst on holiday in France with my wife a couple of years ago. We were lying on sunbeds by the pool, around 10 a.m., waiting for the sunshine and other people to join us when our peace was interrupted by an aerobics class which began on the other side of the pool. Led by the most attractive French couple we'd ever seen, their bodies barely wrapped in Lycra, we both lay transfixed as the music started to pound. Their equally encouraging and teasing commentary began, 'Ouvrez, fermez, ouvrez, fermez ...' as their raised legs opened and closed before our eyes. Our heart rates increased, though not through exercise. 'Ouvrez, fermez, un, deux, trois,' they continued, seductively, to the beat.

Wow, I thought. What a way to learn French. Visual, auditory, kinaesthetic and positive state – all sorted. I can imagine teenage boys across the land collecting their grade 'A' French GCSE barely believing they'd earned it. 'Yes Mum, it was hard work, all that aerobics with Madame Lycra, but I did it for you!'

Now, I know not all teachers look great in Lycra. In fact, you've probably just been put off your next meal by imagining a certain colleague in an all-in-one, skin-tight, blue outfit.

It's difficult to learn anything when only one system is used and we're in a state of boredom, anger or sadness. Yes, we do recall some memories best in one system – faces and maps as pictures, songs by saying them and dance moves by doing them, but we live in a world and in a body that is more complicated than that. We can teach, inspire and motivate people in amazing ways when we use all three major representational systems – that is to say V, A and K – combined with a positive state, and the good news is we don't need to look great in Lycra to achieve this. Controlling our state means we can control our behaviour. This is amazing; we have the HOW to control our behaviour. I know, you may be thinking that's a little greedy, like choosing all the desserts on the menu, but go on, why not?

For more try *5 of Diamonds*, *3 of Hearts*, *Queen of Clubs* and *Ace of Spades*.

Real strategic management

All of our behaviour is the result of the sequences of VAK (and other senses such as taste and smell) we process inside our minds and bodies. These sequences are called 'strategies'. We run strategies for motivation, learning, memory, checking reality and making decisions. Strategies for passing the chip shop or going inside and thousands of others. Many activities in this book explore strategies and how we can 'borrow' effective strategies from other people, something we call 'modelling'.

One of my favourites is the 'copping off' strategy. What happens when we're single and see someone we fancy? Our aim is to go over and talk to the person. What strategy do we run in our head to make us successful – or not – at this activity? In my experience around 80% of people say they're not very good at going over to talk to someone they fancy and 20% say they are good at it. (Just to clarify, I mean without the use of alcohol or drugs. We tend to be less attractive than we think we are when we're drunk, anyway.) Interestingly, the more academic and supposedly clever the group of people are, the less likely they are to be good at this! This has nothing to do with good looks, either, which explains why there are some very ugly people with partners and many attractive single people. A good or bad strategy is defined as whether it gets the result we're after – in other words to talk to the person we fancy.

Ask those not good at going over to talk to the person they fancy what happens and they usually say this:

• They picture or see the person.

- I talk to myself and say things like, 'Ooh they look good, they'll probably not fancy me though, they'll think I've been hit with the ugly stick, I'm not in their league ...'
- It's like they're playing the theme tune to *Jaws* in their head.
- Then they feel nervous.
- They run through a negative VAK sequence until they feel so bad that their exit point is to decide not to talk to the person. They feel temporary relief and then usually berate themselves soon after saying:
- You coward, it could have been the one!

Ask those good at talking to people they fancy and they say things like:

- They picture or see the person.
- They talk to themselves and say things like, 'Ooh, they look good, we could get on well, they could fancy me, we could have an interesting chat, and if we don't get along there are plenty more fish in the sea/shoes in the shop. It's their loss.'
- It's like they're playing the theme to *Rocky* in their heads.
- They then feel confident or go for it.
- They run through this positive VAK sequence until they feel so good that their exit point is to go over and talk to the person they fancy.

You may have noticed the process is very similar but the result very different.

We run similar decision making strategies in other areas of life, such as returning unwanted goods, going to the gym, an interview performance. We can be good at some of these and bad at others because of the strategies we run. You are not a crap person, you may just be using some unhelpful strategies in some parts of your life. This is a great message to pass on to people: 'You're not crap – it's just your strategy.'

We can change our strategies. Sometimes we do it naturally, like people who just get over a phobia or some other negative pattern of behaviour. Charlie Chaplin, proving he knew a bit about NLP as well as being able to fall over humorously, once said: 'Life is a tragedy when seen in close-up, but it's a comedy in long shot.'

Or we can use this knowledge to change our strategies if they are not achieving the results we seek. This is real personal power. It releases us from limiting beliefs and behaviours. This does not mean all people will fancy you, but it does mean you will be able to talk to all the people you fancy.

For more, try *King of Diamonds*, *Ace of Hearts*, *King of Clubs* and *6 of Spades*.

The meta model – a way to turn negative to positive

The meta model is a huge part of NLP. We use words to describe what we mean and feel. However, they are shorthand, they do not convey the complexity of our experience. Sometimes this shorthand causes us problems. Sometimes when we generalise, delete or dis- tort the meaning, we can cause a negative impact. If we say 'Nobody likes me' and believe it to be true we could be causing ourselves unnecessary problems. It is best to challenge the state- ment and recover the lost information:

'Nobody likes me!' (Nobody?)
'Well no one at school' (No one at school?)
'Well no one in my class!' (Really?)
'John Smith said I was a chav!'

One person saying one thing to someone can be generalised into something much bigger. The meta model describes the impact of the way we use words and how they create our subjective experi- ence. In the lower number Diamond cards we discover the impact of the 'meta model' on our beliefs.

Don't doubt the power of these patterns of words, especially from the mouths of teachers. When I was working with adults as a careers adviser, I was often sat in front of someone who would say, 'I'm thick.' When I asked, 'How do you know?' they'd usually say that a teacher told them. They had carried this belief around for many years, unable to progress in their careers or lives. I share this to show how, because teachers have great power when they label children, we should make sure they label them accurately and positively. This way, children can go on and achieve their full potential. A similar example is the influence held by doctors. The power of the placebo effect is well documented.

In his fantastic book, *Bad Science*, Ben Goldacre describes how a Dr Wolf tested the placebo effect to the limit. He told two women suffering from nausea he could relieve their symptoms with a drug, administered via a tube into their stomachs. Both patients improved dramatically. What he hadn't told the women was the drug he administered should have actually made their nausea much worse. His name probably helped too. We generally believe what we're told by authority figures and I've yet to meet someone who hasn't experienced the positive impact of at least one teacher during their education.

Patterns to look for:
The meta model gathers lost information, clarifies meaning, identifies the limits of the originator's statement and increases the number of possible choices we can think about. These are particularly useful when you hear yourself, or others, make negative and debilitating statements. Recognise and challenge the statements using the meta model to help the originator of the statement change their thinking. Then use outcome frame questions (*8 of Clubs*) to move the person forward. Here are some examples (most of them heard in staff rooms) with suggested responses:

Nominalisations (process words frozen in time):
This class is stupid/difficult ...

Ask: What do you mean by stupid/difficult? Always? All of the class?

Outcome Frame: How would you like the class to be? What can you do to move towards this? Who could help you?

Mind-Reading (assuming you know what someone is thinking):
I know you're not interested in Shakespeare/Hockey/keeping the new build new ...

Ask: How do you know? What evidence do you have?

Outcome Frame: What can you do to make them more interested? Who could help you? When by?

Complex Equivalence (linking two unrelated things):
This class makes me angry/will be the death of me ...

Ask: What specifically do they do that makes you think that way? Always?

Outcome Frame: How would you prefer to feel? What can you do to achieve this?

Presuppositions (an implied assumption):
If you knew the importance of school/learning/good behaviour you'd try harder.

Ask: How do you know they don't know the importance?

Outcome Frame: Where do you want to get to with the group? How can you get there?

Universal Quantifiers (universal generalisations):
You always mess around, You're always wrong, You'll never be good at maths, Every year this happens ...

Ask for counter examples, situations when the statement is not true.

Outcome Frame: What can you do to prevent the statement being true? What would you like instead? What specifically makes some children become better at maths? Could we use that knowledge?

Modal Operators (words that mark out a belief):
You can't sing/draw/do sport, you have to do this, I can't help you, You shouldn't/mustn't ...

Ask: What would happen if you could/did? Clarify the belief behind the statement, Whose belief is it? What is the impact of this belief?

Outcome Frame: Is the belief helpful or not? If not, what can be done to give the person more control/choice?

Lost Performative (value judgment made without a specified originator):

This is a bad/failing year/group/class/school/department/Head ...

Ask: For the originator of the statement, How do they know?

Outcome Frame: What judgment is preferred? (e.g. excellent rather than bad). How can we get there?

Deletions (information missing from statement):

I'm uncomfortable with this, She's better than me, This class/year is worse than the last year, You don't care about me, They never listen to me.

Ask: For the missing information. Uncomfortable about what/whom? Better than what/whom? In what way worse?

Outcome Frame: What would you like to happen? How can you/we make it happen? When by?

Whoever said 'Sticks and stones will break my bones but words will never hurt me,' was wrong. Words are powerful and the meta model helps us recover the meaning behind the words precisely. When combined with the Milton Model below you can become an alchemist of words.

The Milton Model – a way to develop positive behaviour

Milton Erickson, a world-renowned medical hypnotist, was a huge influence on NLP. He believed that people make the best choices available to them at the time, have the answers and resources within to make the desired change, and that a positive intent drives all behaviours. You may have already noticed that the structure of this book is based around these ideas. Milton used artfully vague language to unleash unconscious potential. The depth of Milton's skill is well illustrated in books such as *My Voice Will Go With You*, by Sidney Rosen and *The User's Manual for the Brain*, by Bob Bodenhamer and Michael Hall.

We can use the same patterns as described above in the meta model, but we can use **positive** language to develop empowering states and beliefs.

As you've been good, here is a Bonus Activity: A fascinating activity is to take your star signs from a newspaper and ask people to find the Milton patterns used in the infamously vague language employed. What information is missing in your own stars? This can be great fun. It reveals how the Milton model – the artful and positive use of vague language – can be used to ensure people make sense of the information and relate it personally and purposefully to their own lives.

Bonus Activity for Good Teachers: Star Sign

Time: 20 mins

Activity: Find Milton Model patterns (described below) in your stars for today, available in most tabloids.

Here is an example of the Milton Model in the world of horoscopes and the Miltonian descriptions of what's going on:

Taurus: A load of bull?

I know you are ready (mind reading – how could you know?) for a better time (deletion – better than what, when, whom?).

Hesitation annoys you (cause-effect – link two unrelated things) and with Venus in Uranus you need to seize the opportunity (complex equivalence – link two different experiences. Are these two things really linked?).

because everyone wants to be their best (universal quantifier – we can't speak for everyone).

The fun of this activity is to identify how we take language for granted and make meaning from it that affects us, our beliefs and even our destiny.

A second optional part to *Star Sign* activity (30 mins) is to use Milton patterns to develop 'scripts' you can use with your students to enhance their motivation. For example:

> 'I know (mind reading) you are a good person (deletion), you have maybe just made some bad decisions (deletion) in the past. This school wants you to do your best (deletion) and we both know (mind reading) you can do much better (deletion) than you have done this week. You can make good decisions (modal operator), I've seen you do well, the work you produced on the school trip made me proud of you (complex equivalence). You can make yourself proud by putting the silly stuff behind you (deletion) and looking at what you can achieve (modal operator) ... '

Although researchers have assessed the impact of NLP within education, it's often on the bits easiest to measure, such as eye accessing cues and assessing VAK preferences, rather than the bits that could have the biggest impact, such as the activities within this book. A good example of research looking at the impact of the Milton Model in education is highlighted in Cialdini's book *Influence: The Psychology of Persuasion*. Students were split into two groups. One group was told by the teacher: practice your handwriting; the other group told: you seem to me to be children that understand the importance of neat handwriting. The second group practiced their handwriting more than the first group, even though they weren't specifically told to do so. Can you identify the language patterns used? Have a go and then check below:

You seem to me (mind reading, *how do you know?*) to be children that understand the importance of neat hand writing (pre-supposition, *assumption that neat hand writing is important is made*).

Here are further examples of Milton Model language – deliberately vague language for positive outcomes:

Deletions

You're comfortable, your best is yet to come, you're a great group, young people are naturally great learners, we are here to develop your learning, using your curiosity to reduce difficulty, you want to learn.

Cause-Effect

As you sit here you will become more focused on today's work.
Relaxing improves our concentration.
The more you listen the more you'll understand.

Mind Reading

We're here for a reason.
You may be wondering what we'll be learning today.
I know which parts of this subject you like best.
I know how hard you've worked so far this term.
I know you think about your future.

Lost Performative

It's good you can learn so easily.
It's important to do your best.

Universal Quantifiers

Always ask if you don't understand.
All teenage brains have huge potential.
We want you all to achieve your best.

Modal Operators

You can enjoy school.
You can do more than you think.
You mustn't listen to the media saying negative things about teenagers.

Presuppositions

Fortunately, as you're interested in better ways of doing well in this subject, you'll learn more quickly now and be more successful all the way through your life.

Stack some of these together for an effective 'horoscope' for all your students. Remember to be positive in approach and voice. You should only say things you believe to be true.

For example:

I know (1) this is a good class (2) because (3) I've taught many classes and I know (1) you can (4) all (5) be really successful in the future (2).

(1) Mind Reading

(2) Deletion

(3) Cause-Effect

(4) Modal Operator

(5) Universal Quantifier

And more: Can you spot the patterns this time?

'I enjoy teaching bright motivated classes and have been pleased and surprised at the high quality of work produced so far, keep it up everyone and we'll have a great year. I know you know, deep down, that you can have a successful adult life, you are building foundations here, think about what you can achieve if you do your best and we will help you work towards your goals. The more you believe in yourself and know your strengths the better you'll be able to plan your future success. I want you to become confident young adults ready to go for it and achieve like so many of the students we have supported in this school.'

Using Milton patterns of language is particularly effective with individuals you know well because you can link past achievements to a positive future and the steps required over the next few months.

Logical Levels

Another useful area of NLP was initiated by Robert Dilts. He developed the concept of Logical Levels. Simply, we function at different levels, all equally important but reflecting different aspects of who we are, like a Russian doll. Recognising the level at which someone is functioning can help us target our support more effectively. All of the Hearts card activities apply the principles of logical levels.

This is a simplified version of logical levels.

We function at all of these levels:

1. Identity (the who): 'I'm just not *that* kind of person and *that* dress is just not me.' Our identity underpins our life. When we're fulfilled it creates deep happiness and contentment; when inhibited it causes deep dissatisfaction. The following words may help you define your identity. Which words are you attracted to? Which words resonate deeply: Advocate, Adviser, Artist, Athlete, Coach, Counsellor, Comedian, Crafter, Creator, Discoverer, Explorer, Firefighter, Healer, Hunter, Improviser, Inspector, Inventor, Leader, Learner, Magician, Mediator, Mentor, Organiser, Performer, Promoter, Protector, Provider, Sage (wise person), Saint, Supervisor, Teacher, Warrior, Parent, Child, Sibling, Husband/Wife. These final three are worth avoiding: Victim, Villain, Hero/Heroine.

Discovering our own identity can be fascinating but assigning identity to groups can be even more intriguing. Politicians grapple with what it is to be British, European, white, black, etc. Religions, families, schools, too, search for a collection of ideas, beliefs and values to bind them together and provide a sense of purpose and direction. In my own family I have experienced the difficulty of defining our group identity.

Bonus Activity for Good Teachers: Logical Levels

Use your school as a case study to explore all logical levels. Consider the identity of your school. Identity is often enshrined in the vision statements of an organisation or in a school motto. (Although often the real identity of an organisation is different to the publicised identity.) What is the real motto of your school? 'SATS R US'? 'Sit down and shut up'? 'Everyone can be their best'? Next, consider the personality of your school, the natural strengths of the staff and students? What skills does your school need to use or develop to achieve the identity to which you aspire? Then, what behaviour is required by staff and students to make these happen? Finally, what environment would best serve the development of the school towards the above goals?

When I was a child I was working class, as an adult probably middle class. What about my children? I sought evidence. Sunday family trips to that bastion of middle class, middle-Englandness – the National Trust property – suggested they were *not* middle class. As the children of other families skipped merrily and respectfully around the property filling in their photocopied sheets and announcing with alacrity, 'Look Mummy, I've found the William Morris fuchsia design,' my children trudged reluctantly to the gift shop hoping for more than a room packed with over-priced stationery, educational toys and over-packaged jam. ('Educational toy' is code for 'overpriced wooden trinket from sustainable woodland that provides no more than four minutes of interesting play time.') So, no, they aren't middle class, but the definition of who we are is important, as it is the invisible compass that guides us, as individuals and as groups.

2. Personality (the why): the inbuilt natural strengths and characteristics we all have that are relatively stable and unchanging throughout our lives, which is why it is very useful for us to know what these are.

Which of these reflect your personality: Achiever, Analytical, Caring, Determined, Enthusiastic, Flexible, Friendly, Funny, Generous, Imaginative, Independent, Loyal, Modest, Organised, Practical.

3. Capability (the how): The skills we learn. Beliefs and values are examples of 'learned' patterns of thought, usually coded through our internal dialogue, 'I can't, I can ...' sing, draw, keep a partner, be happy. Does your internal dialogue mostly help or hinder you? Skills such as driving and sport are usually coded through muscle memory; practice makes (towards) perfect. Multiple intelligences are a great framework enabling people to identify the skills they possess and can develop. In his book *Outliers*, Malcolm Gladwell explores how exceptional achievers reach the top of their field. He suggests that to be really skilled to the level of expert requires around 10,000 hours of practice.

4. Behaviour and Mood (the what): Our thoughts and actions. What are they achieving or not achieving for us? What behaviour is most likely going to help us achieve our aims: Autonomy, Bravery, Caring, Elegance, Excitement, Fairness, Fun, Grace, Helping, Honesty, Humour, Innovation, Joy, Learning, Love, Organised, Originality, Passion, Perseverance, Play, Security, Self-reliance, Service, Simplicity, Problem Solving, Uniqueness, Vitality, Wisdom, Zest, Positive, Happy, Buzzing, Confident Learner, Curious, Relaxed, Miserable, Sad, Angry, Friendly, Hesitant, Confused, Bored, Jealous

Habits become behaviour.

There have been many studies on the habits of successful people in life, business, relationships, parenting, generating wealth and others.

For those in work I suggest they consider the following behaviours as ways to make more of their work (for more see *The Art of Building Windmills* by Peter Hawkins):

Learn from others, start noticing why some people get on and others don't. What behaviour is rewarded? Could you behave in

195

the same way? If some people seem good at tasks could you ask them how they do it?

Promote yourself, Don't brag but do take the credit for your good ideas and success. Put forward your ideas, especially those that save company time and money. Be positive and friendly because it spreads. Look for ways to solve problems, not just talking about them.

Offer to help, talk to your boss about how you can help the business. Could you do some research with customers or suppliers? Could you take on additional roles or responsibilities?

5. Environment (the where and when): Ever been in the right place at the right time (or wrong place, wrong time)? Where we frequent determines the people we meet. This has a major impact on our lives. In a work context it is called networking. For children, their schools and neighbourhoods can have a major impact on their health and wealth. What places will help ensure more of the good 'stuff' happens in their lives?

Callers to a radio phone-in show were asked how they met their partners. One woman said she had been between boyfriends for too long. I think she meant without a boyfriend rather than being in a ménage à trois. She thought about the kind of boyfriend she would like and decided as follows – age: mid 20s, build: strong and muscular, interests: sporty. She thought about where she could meet such a bloke and took a job as a part-time barmaid at the local rugby club. She had quite a choice and is now happily married. She knew the importance of environment. If I know my stereotypes, then I reckon if she'd worked at a bookshop, taken up pottery or joined the National Trust she'd have met different types of men.

To achieve rapport, peace, nirvana, happiness (or whatever you want to call it) then complete each level. When we know ourselves at all of these levels we can become our best. If not, we're a ship sailing without a destination, drifting randomly.

Questions to ask yourself:

If you were being your most successful where and with whom would you spend more time?

With which people and in which places would you spend less time than you do now if you want to be really successful?

What courses, social networks, clubs, societies or groups could you join to meet people that could positively help you move on in your life?

Our capacity to live in tune with our sense of identity will allow us to make a positive impact in the world.

Suggested lesson plans:

For a 20-30 minute motivational session:
Choose the same four numbers, one from each suit, deliver in the order Diamonds, Hearts, Clubs, Spades and you will take the students through all four cycles.

For PHSE:
Cards 8 and 9 of each suit.

For SEAL:
Jack & Queen of each suit.
For a half day with a whole year group in tables to compete against each other:

Magic

Queen of Spades (tested at end of session)

Ace of Diamonds

8 of Diamonds

9 of Diamonds

2 through to 8 of Hearts

3 of Clubs (teachers to award points per table)

4 of Clubs

5 of Clubs

King of Spades

For INSET (two half days):

2 of Diamonds

King of Hearts

Ace of Clubs

3 of Spades

5 of Diamonds

3 of Hearts

Bonus Activity Card 1 King of Diamonds

Ace of Hearts

King of Clubs

6 of Spades & Bonus Activity Card 2

Splash Zone Activity.

Here are some additional activities to use with students for a big start or finale.

Could it be Magic?

OK, it's not really magic but I was brought up watching the *Paul Daniels Magic Show* on TV and it did me no harm. Well, not a lot. I always thought the joke, 'I didn't get into magic when I was young, I had friends instead' was a bit cruel. In my experience a few 'illusions' can help a session rattle along. Especially if you don't tell the audience how it's done until the end of the session and only then if there's time. There are many books and internet sites you can plunder for card tricks. I'm avoiding them myself, which you may think odd considering the format of this book; instead I'll describe a couple of my favourites that are on a bigger scale, more visual and involve audience participation. Card tricks work best in small groups; the following activities in large groups.

Turning water into wine?

Effect:
You say you can turn a glass of water into 10 different drinks. You show a list with 10 drinks written out: tea, coffee, milk, lemonade, cola, beer, wine, orange juice, blackcurrant and whisky. You invite two students from the audience to join you. Ask for students with a good sense of smell.

You take a bottle of pre-bought water, unopened. Ask one of the volunteers to pour it out into a clear glass, both of them to smell it and verify it is water. You can even invite some of the audience to smell it. Ask them not to drink it for health/safety/germs reasons. You then take the glass, stare at the volunteers, ask them to concentrate, and say you are going to turn the water into one of the liquids on the list. Just before you put the glass down. You hand them a sheet of folded paper. Ask, 'Are you ready? Sure? OK let's go for it.'

You wave the glass in front of their noses and ask what is it?

They reply, 'Lemonade!' And the audience laughs. Ask, 'Are you sure?' 'Yes,' they confirm. You can add a joke, 'So it's not beer?' (the Paul Daniels show may have gone but his humour lives on). You then ask the volunteer to unfold the piece of paper you gave and show it to the audience revealing the word 'Lemonade'. Thank the volunteers and invite them to return to their seats.

The trick!
You place lemon balm plant leaves in one trouser pocket.
When you handle the glass at the end of the trick you use the hand which you've had in this pocket (don't make it obvious) so they smell your fingers, not the liquid.
The rest of the time use you other hand. Lemon balm leaves are so strong that this will work effectively. People look for you to tamper with the water and don't suspect the truth.

Body Language/Mind Reader?

Effect:

Say you're going to read minds.

You ask for five volunteers to sit in chairs in a line. Each is given an identical pen or pencil, sheet of blank paper and an envelope. Ask them to write down three things you couldn't possibly know about them, but that some people in the audience will know. Offer suggestions, such as the name of their pet dog, sister, the street they live in, team they support, favourite food, band, colour, etc. Help by saying make it hard for me, don't write stuff I could easily guess; if one of them is wearing a ring with the name of a band on it, they shouldn't write down the name. You move away so you can't see what they're writing.

When finished, they place the papers in the envelopes, and while they are doing it, you could talk to the audience about mind reading, reading body language, especially if you are going to do activities next that involve these subjects. You could also say that your chances of guessing correctly the information on all five volunteers are 5 X 4 X 3 X 2 = 120 to 1.

They should seal the envelopes and get someone to collect them and mix them up before passing them to you.

You open envelopes one at a time and correctly identify each person.

The trick!

Before you start you mark the envelopes 1 to 5. Choose envelopes that have very similar size flaps, that are easily opened and re-sealed, and write the number inside the sealed end. Give out the envelopes in the order that the five participants are sitting. Tell them to seal the envelope at one end, but you open it at the other, revealing the number and identifying the person. You have to be a little theatrical and pretend you're having to concentrate and study their body language, look into their soul etc to make it convincing. On the third envelope it's a good idea to guess just by feeling the sheet of paper without even looking at the clues then hand it to the person and ask if it is theirs and they'll be a little spooked!

Mad Maths!

Effect:
Ask for two volunteers who are excellent at maths.
Once they're with you 'on stage' check that they are good at maths.
Sit them either side of the stage on a chair facing the audience.
Say you're going to give them £25 for each sum they add correctly; each sum is two three-digit numbers. They have to work it out in their head and both have to guess correctly in six seconds per sum. They can split the money how they want but it will be £50 in total. Ask how they'd like to split it. This leads to an easy joke about their mathematical prowess. You show each person the same sum written on A4 paper and then ask both to write down their answer. You show the audience the sheet and then ask the volunteers to reveal their answers. One will be correct, the other wrong. You repeat the exercise and this time the other person gets it right but the other gets it wrong. You keep your £50.

The trick!
The sums (additions) are written as follows:

$$8\ 0\ 8 \qquad 6\ 0\ 9$$
$$1\ 6\ 1 \qquad 8\ 1\ 1$$

You present the sheet upside down to one of the volunteers, which means they will produce a different answer. Note: the typeface means the 1 is not the same upside down, you need to draw the number so they look the same both ways or it is a terrible trick!
Explain the trick immediately, because you don't want to make the volunteers look bad. Explain you only did it to show that those people who think they are bad at maths often think it means they're stupid people. Many believe this until they die!

Illiteracy and innumeracy are a double blight on people's lives because they often label themselves as stupid as well as not being able to do basic maths and read or write.

Before you go

The Splash Zone

During our first family holiday in Florida we went to SeaWorld where my daughter didn't go on many of the rides. I knew she wanted to, but she was afraid. The second time, two years later, she did. As we stood nervously in the queues, she was running through in her head what might happen to her on the ride. I was wondering if she would bottle out and make us walk back through the line we joined 20 minutes ago. After the rides, my daughter was so pleased with herself she said, 'That was brilliant, can we go on again?'

The funniest was the Splash Zone for Shamu Rocks at SeaWorld. The audience was split into those people heading straight for the Splash Zone, the reticent wanting to sit in the Splash Zone, and those not wanting to be anywhere near the fun (they're the ones who spend their holiday behind a video recorder, never in the experience, just watching it as a detached critic). Yes, this is supposed to be a metaphor! In which group do you live your life? 'Shall we go in the Splash Zone?' my daughter asked with a little twinkle in her eye. Go on then. We did and we got wet and we laughed and we still laugh about it now.

I've researched pleasure in books and in real life*, and one definition stands out above the rest. Stephen Fry describes pleasure as experiencing 'something that is better than it has to be'. A meal, journey, conversation, etc. The example he offered was Abba. They were far better than they needed to be. They could have been as good as a-ha and that would have been perfectly satisfactory;

---

* More in the former than the latter, but I'm learning the latter is the place to be!

instead they were brilliant and have left a legacy of fantastic pop music. In most areas of life perfectly satisfactory is perfectly satisfactory. In education it is not; the stakes are too high, the prize too important. Go and bring some Abba into your classroom and life ... outfit optional.

The Splash Zone
Time: 5 mins

Activity: After sharing the above story I demonstrate the highlights of the Shamu show with a small toy killer whale. I produce a water pistol and spray parts of the group. This works best in very large groups, otherwise it could be seen as victimisation. I invite them to stand up and enjoy the experience, because if they're hit with water it proves they are alive. I suggest those people who join in with this activity are more likely to have a full and successful life because they've got the right attitude.

If you're not into a big finish you can select another activity.

Learning Point: Sometimes it's best not to say; each person will create their own meaning from the activity.

Preparation: A killer whale, water pistol, a little water, Abba music, outfit optional.

Bibliography

Andreas, S and Faulkner, C *NLP: The New Technology of Achievement*, Nicholas Brealey, London, 1996.

Bannatyne, D *Wake Up and Change Your Life*, Orion, London, 2008.

Battino, R *Expectation, The Very Brief Therapy Book*, Crown House Publishing, Carmarthen, 2008.

Bodenhamer, B and Hall L M *The Users Manual for the Brain*, Crown House Publishing, Carmarthen, 2003.

Boldstad, R *Resolve: A New Model of Therapy*, Crown House Publishing, Carmarthen, 2002.

Branson, R *Losing My Virginity*, Virgin Books, London, 2002.

Brown, D *Tricks of the Mind*, Random House, London, 2006.

Charvet, S R *Words that Change Minds*, Kendall/Hunt, 1997.

Cialdini, R *Influence: The Psychology of Persuasion*, Profile, London 2007.

Claxton, G *What's the Point of School?, 2008, OneWorld*

Covey, S *The Seven Habits of Highly Effective People*, Simon & Schuster, London, 1999.

Csikszentmihalyi, M *Flow*, Random House, London, 2002.

Curran, A *The Little Book of Big Stuff About the Brain*, Crown House Publishing, Carmarthen, 2008.

Dennis, F *How to Get Rich,* Random House, London, 2007.

Feinstein, S *The Secrets of the Teenage Brain,* Sage, London, 2004.

Foster R, Hicks G *How We Choose to Be Happy*, Perigee, New York, 1999.

Fulves, K *Self-Working Mental Magic*, Dover, New York, 1979.

Gardner, H *Frames of Mind*, Fontana, London, 1993.

Gatto, J T *Dumbing Us Down*, New Society, 2005.

Gilbert, D *Stumbling on Happiness*, Harper Perennial, 2007.

Gilbert, I *Essential Motivation in the Classroom*, Routledge, London, 2002.

Gilbert, I (Ed) *The Big Book of Independent Thinking*, Crown House Publishing, Carmarthen, 2006.

Gilbert, I *The Little Book of Thunks®*, Crown House Publishing, Carmarthen, 2007.

Ginnis, P *The Teacher's Toolkit*, Crown House Publishing, Carmarthen, 2001.

Goldstein, N J, Martin, S J and Cialdini, R B *Yes! The Secret Science of Persuasion*, Profile, London, 2007.

Goldacre, B *Bad Science*, Fourth Estate, London, 2008.

Handy, C *The Hungry Spirit*, Arrow, London, 1998.

Hatcher, T *Burnt Toast*, Harper, London, 2007.

Hawkins, P *The Art of Building Windmills*, Graduate into Employment Unit, University of Liverpool, 1999.

Hodgson, D *The Buzz: A Practical Confidence Builder for Teenagers*, Crown House Publishing, Carmarthen, 2006.

Hoggard, L *How to Be Happy*, BBC Books, London, 2005.

Holt, J *How Children Learn*, Penguin, London, 1991.

Jackson, N *The Little Book of Music in the Classroom*, Crown House Publishing, Carmarthen, 2009.

James, T and Shephard, D *Presenting Magically*, Crown House Publishing, Carmarthen, 2002.

Johnson, S *Who Moved My Cheese?*, Vermilion, 1999.

Bibliography

Jensen, E *Super Teaching*, The Brain Store Inc, 1998.

Leighton, R *Success in the Creative Classroom*, Network Continuum Education, 2007.

Lester, D *How They Started*, Crimson, 2007.

Lunden, S C, Paul H, and Christensen J *Fish Omnibus*, Hodder & Stoughton, London, 2006.

McKenna, P *I Can Make You Rich*, Bantam, London, 2007.

Maconie, S *Pies and Prejudice*, Random House, London, 2008.

O'Brien, D *How to Develop a Brilliant Memory*, Duncan Baird, 2005.

Pease, A & B *The Definitive Book of Body Language*, Orion, London, 2005.

Pert, C *Molecules of Emotion*, Pocket Books, 1999.

Philips, A *Darwin's Worms*, Faber and Faber, 1999.

Robinson, K *Out of Our Minds*, Capstone, 2001.

Rosen, S *My Voice Will Go with You*, W W Norton & Co, 1991.

Tieger, P and Baron, B *Do What You Are*, Little, Brown & Company, 2001.

Praise for *The Little Book of Inspirational Teaching Activities*

As an Inset Coordinator I could fill a year's worth of training for teachers using these techniques alone and the best thing is they transcend all curriculum areas.

From the minute I picked it up I couldn't put it down. It is easy to understand every section and to visualise how to use it with young people. Particularly good use of humour, it was actually fun to read.

In the teaching world it is so difficult to grab extra time to do anything new and this is the beauty of the book, you don't need extra time, you can easily incorporate the activities into everyday delivery as they only take as long as a typical registration period.

After reading this book anyone would have to agree the world of teaching and training is a better place for having David Hodgson in it. The work he produces is not only inspirational to professionals but it actually does what it says on the cover, it works with young people.

Yvonne Haymonds, Curriculum Co ordinator,
Connexions Hub Services in Tyne and Wear

I have known David for many years, meeting him regularly at Institute of Career Guidance conferences, taking part in his workshops or just listening to his enthusiasm and motivations for NLP and how to get people to believe in their own potential.

Most of my own work involves motivating prisoners and ex-offenders to believe they have skills and abilities that will support them to reintegrate back into the community in a positive way, to find employment and also to learn. I believe these activities can help people who have negative experiences of education and who consider themselves unemployable. Many of the activities will enable them to realise that they have skills to offer employers and also the ability to learn new things. Enabling people to realise they have potential, which helps them to cope with whatever is thrown at them, is very powerful.

Many prisoners and ex-offenders see themselves as a product of their environment. "I didn't want to be a product of my environment – I want my environment to be a product of me" will work very powerfully on them.

What I have enjoyed most of all is the introductions and explanations to the four suits and each activity. The information makes you smile and gives you confidence to go and have a go with different activities. It is like a ready reckoner of activities that can be easily integrated into any lessons or training programmes.

Jo Noblett, Senior Executive - Employability for Offenders, Careers Scotland

This is a superb little book, packed full of interesting and engaging activities for teachers or anyone working in groups with young people. It comprises of four main sections or 'themes': Believe in Yourself, Know Your Strengths, Have a Plan and Go for it! The activities can either be translated into an entire programme for confidence building, self-esteem and motivation, or they can be delivered on a 'stand alone' basis.

Each activity is preceded by a short introductory paragraph, which sets the activity in context and provides useful background information. The instructions for the activities are easy to follow and outline key learning points and associated resources. Although many of the activities don't actually require any pre-prepared resources.

All the activities are designed to get pupils thinking creatively – allowing them to tap into their inner resources but have fun at the same time.

David also provides a thought-provoking introduction, which he calls 'Rules of Inspiration'. This reminds us of the fundamental principles of effective teaching and learning and challenges us to make our sessions engaging, interesting and above all, enjoyable.

The final chapter provides a short but coherent overview of some of the main NLP presuppositions and how they can be applied in practice. There is also a very interesting and useful Bibliography provided.

As with David's previous book, *The Buzz*, the author sets out a simple, easy to understand and practical application of NLP and shows how it can be used to maximise potential and motivate young people to achieve their goals.

In my role as Senior Lecturer on the Postgraduate Diploma in Careers Guidance at Manchester Metropolitan University, I train future Career Guidance professionals. This year, we included many of David's suggested exercises from *The Little Book of Inspirational Teaching Activities* in the Group Work Training Module, so that new practitioners could invigorate their school work with more lively, student-centred sessions. The activities have proven to be a great success – helping practitioners to engage effectively with young people in groups and getting the pupils to 'think outside the box' and participate fully in the learning experience.

This is a great way of making NLP techniques and solution-focused approaches accessible to practitioners/teachers and young people alike.

Michaela Gill, Senior Lecturer, Postgraduate Diploma in
Careers Guidance, Manchester Metropolitan University

David's book is very useful indeed – an ideal guide for teachers who want to use NLP in the classroom but aren't sure how to start. The format of short, sharp activities means that they can be easily incorporated into lessons or brought together into a sustained programme. Ideal for use in PSHE or as part of the new KS3 curriculum for Personal Learning and Thinking Skills, but with a range of applications across different subjects, particularly as starter activities. What's more, they actually work – having tried some of his ideas in the past I have seen them make a real difference to under aspiring students.

David's style is very readable and engaging. I like the way the activities are organised using the conceit of a deck of cards. I look forward to putting some of it into practice!

Kath Bennett, Assistant Headteacher, Sunnydale Community College

Working with young people who face a multitude of difficult personal issues and who have barriers to succeeding in their lives requires the use of a range of innovative strategies by the professional workers who support them. It is essential therefore that resources developed to support such strategies are clear and simple to use and have a clarity of purpose that the worker fully understands and accepts conceptually.

The Little Book of Inspirational Teaching Activities succeeds in providing easy and effective activities that can be used in a variety of settings and with a wide range of young people. The introduction succinctly affirms the purpose of the book in an accessible style and gains rapid acceptance of the rationale and concepts behind the practical activities. It is this immediate "buy in" to the need to use the techniques to unlock the potential of young people in the introduction, that is the "ace card" of this resource.

The use of playing cards as a vehicle for the key themes of the activities is clear and memorable and provides a practical structure for the wealth of activities contained within each section of the book.

I have taken the opportunity to encourage a number of colleagues who are working directly with young people to use a range of the activities contained in the book in their day to day work. Feedback has been consistently positive with workers and young people alike enjoying the experience. Often the time available to work with individual and groups of young people is limited by the need to work with increasingly high volumes, particularly in areas of high social deprivation. The activities contained in the book are designed to provide quick, enjoyable and stimulating inputs that facilitate their practical use even in a challenging environment. Longer sessions can be developed by combining activities in such a way as to meet individual and group needs. The permutations are seemingly inexhaustible. As with all such resources, colleagues appear to find favourite activities that they can build into the normal repertoire of techniques they use in their daily working practice.

I can recommend this book to anyone working with young people who wants an effective and easy to use manual of enjoyable and stimulating activities at their disposal.

David Hobbs, CEO of the Connexions services in Manchester,
Salford, Tameside and Rochdale

I am not trained in NLP, although I have had some experience of it gained by running events for Topher Morrison Inc and attending a seminar by Tony Robbins. I find that NLP adopts a masculine approach of explaining things logically and tangibly through the use of language. I have seen variable results in people's lives and, despite the marketing, I do not believe it is the cure all and end all of systems in terms of being able to understand the human psyche.

Having said that, the value of NLP in education is something that I can definitely appreciate because teachers who are trained in NLP will be able to 'read' their students in a far more practical way than educators of the past and thereby connect to them as people, hence creating a feeling of caring between student and teacher. More than half the problems in communication stem from expecting others to communicate in the style we feel most comfortable with. NLP is very good for assisting people to appreciate other modalities.

The exercises that appear in this book are innovative as well as using some well tried and tested ones with a different approach. The thing I like about the philosophy of the book is that it is focusing more on emotional intelligence than just facts and figures to pass an exam. It is encouraging teachers to spend some time in each lesson building emotional intelligence in four prime areas of ourselves, namely self esteem (belief in the self); knowing strengths and weaknesses (ability to be part of a team by focusing on strengths and improving weaknesses or allowing someone with strengths that are your weaknesses to do the job); learning to plan for success and having the ability to take a leap of faith without trying to control the outcome.

I really enjoyed paging through the book looking at the learning point, finding one that really resonated with me and then reading the exercise and finding myself smiling at how simple it is to engage the self in learning when one understands the WHY. With much subject-based teaching, there is no 'why' to learning, whereas this book helps the educator explain to the students why one is doing the exercise and the overall result they are aiming for.

I will definitely be recommending different exercises to my adult students who sign up for learning how to learn as part of their own learning and to help their interaction with their study buddies and/or children.

Kate Ginn, Life Long Learner and Author of 'The Secret Learning Code'

I love this book. I love the size of it (just the right size to sneak into a handbag or briefcase), I love the feel of it (strange thing to say about a book, but as soon as you have it in your hands, you'll know exactly what I mean). But, most of all, I love the content.

It is indeed a book of inspirational teaching activities – 'inspirational' being the operative word. The activities are divided up like a pack of cards – the activities in the 'diamond' section are all focussed on Believe in Yourself, the 'hearts' – Know Your Strengths', 'clubs' – Have a Plan, 'Spades' – Go For It. There's even some fun activities in the 'Joker' section, and a useful end section that covers NLP basics and how they can be applied in the classroom.

The activities in the book are explained in simple terms, and each is prefaced with a little anecdote to illustrate why the activity is useful and what you will learn.

Whenever I work in schools or with groups of hard-to-engage learners, (or even with eager, motivated, real workshop-attending, fee-paying adults) I always slip this book into my bag. Why? Because I know that if I dry up, if I run out of steam, if I can't think of what to do for the last half hour, or if there are issues that require attention, I can dip into my Little Blue Book. And, believe me, the answer is always there.

Whether you know nothing about NLP or are a seasoned expert, this book will not disappoint. It is funny, it is informative, it is packed with useful activities (some of them you could even try out at kiddies' parties!), and everyone who works with groups of people of any age should have this book tucked away somewhere, for those moments when you need to inject a little more fun/activity/inspiration/humour/positivity/team spirit into your work.

BUY IT NOW!

Amanda Lowe, Author

More Little Books ...

**The Book of Thunks®: Is not going fishing a hobby?
and other possibly impossible questions to stretch your brain
and annoy your friends**
by Ian Gilbert ISBN: 9781845900922

**The Little Book of Thunks®:
260 questions to make your brain go ouch!**
by Ian Gilbert ISBN: 9781845900625

Little Owl's Book of Thinking
by Ian Gilbert ISBN: 9781904424352

**The Little Book of Big Stuff About the Brain: The true story of
your amazing brain**
by Andrew Curran edited by Ian Gilbert ISBN: 9781845900854

The Little Book of Music for the Classroom
by Nina Jackson edited by Ian Gilbert ISBN: 9781845900915

**The Little Book of Values: Educating children to become
thinking, responsible and caring citizens**
by Julie Duckworth edited by Ian Gilbert ISBN: 9781845901356

Also by David Hodgson

The Buzz: A practical confidence builder for teenagers
by David Hodgson ISBN: 9781904424819

The Little Book of Charisma: Applying the Art and Science
David Hodgson edited by Ian Gilbert ISBN: 978-184590293-3

Magic of Modern Metaphor: Walking with Stars
by David Hodgson edited by Nick Owen ISBN: 978-1845903947